Psychological Yearbook

Psychological Yearbook

University of Copenhagen

Vol. 1 · 1994

Edited by

*Niels Engelsted, Judy Gammelgaard,
Anker Helms Jørgensen, Simo Køppe, Aksel Mortensen*

MUSEUM TUSCULANUM PRESS

Psychological Yearbook Vol. 1
© Museum Tusculanum Press 1994
Layout: Ole Klitgaard
Printed in Denmark by AiO Tryk a-s, Odense
ISSN 1395 0878
ISBN 87 7289 331 1

Published with the support of
The Faculty for the Humanities, University of Copenhagen

MUSEUM TUSCULANUM PRESS
University of Copenhagen
Njalsgade 92
DK-2300 Copenhagen S.
Denmark

TABLE OF CONTENTS

Niels Engelsted & Simo Køppe: Placing Copenhagen Psychology
on the map – A sketch of its history and present state 9

Judy Gammelgaard: Psychoanalysis and classical tragedy 27

Arne Friemuth Petersen: Biopsychological aspects of individuation:
on the origin of and interplay between biological
individuality, personality and self 45

Ole Dreier: Personal locations and perspectives – Psychological
aspects of social practice 63

Publications 1992-1993 by Researchers at Psychological Laboratory,
Institute of Clinical Psychology, University of Copenhagen 91

Foreword

University of Copenhagen is 515 years old and *psychology* as an autonomous department in this university is 108 years old.

We have two institutes – Psychological Laboratory and Institute of Clinical Psychology – with 50 researchers and 1500 students.

In the last decade of the twentieth century internationalization is an increasing demand and in that perspective we have decided to begin the publishing of a psychological yearbook from Copenhagen.

In the first volume we shortly present our history in the first chapter and then give place for presentations of three (doctor phil.) theses published in 1993.

If you in a single word should characterize Copenhagen-Psychology the word should be multiplicity. Many psychological schools and scientific traditions are represented; that means existence of traditional as well as current scientific educational and practice-inspired fields of problems as focus for research.

It is our hope that these presentations tell the readers about original and solid research built upon an innovative tradition, a legacy from experimental psychology and a phenomenological tradition through 100 years. In our opinion it is due to this tradition that psychology has avoided the empiristic as well as the subjectivistic pitfall.

We are looking forward to communication and co-operation with new research-fellows through this publication.

Aksel Mortensen
Head of Psychological Laboratory

Judy Gammelgaard
Head of Institute of Clinical Psychology

Placing Copenhagen Psychology on the map

– A sketch of its history and present state

NIELS ENGELSTED & SIMO KØPPE

The roots

Denmark lies at a crossroads between North and South and East and West, and this position has shaped the Danish intellectual landscape. Ideas follow trade routes, and the Danish marketplace has been a meeting place for all the major intellectual trends in philosophy and science. To prevent it turning into a battlefield too, there has always been an interest in possible compromises or the striking of deals; and when the major "isms" proved uncompromising, a readiness to shift the focus to the more subjective stance of the individual. And there has always been a keen eye for the pragmatic.

Pluralism, synthesis, pragmatism, and a penchant for the subjective have been recurrent themes in the development of Danish psychology from the very beginning. Johann Nicolai Tetens, professor at Kiel and later Copenhagen, is a case in point. He tried to reconcile rationalism and empiricism and has won a name in the annals for originating in 1777 the tripartite division of psychological phenomena into conative, cognitive and affective that Immanuel Kant adopted as basis for his three Critiques.[1] Kant, however, did not care for Tetens' experimental investigations of perception, claiming in principle that the inner sense could not be subjected to quantification and empirical procedure. Due to the influence of Kant, Tetens' new method therefore did not catch on, and the introduction of experiment in psychological inquiry had to await the work of the German physiologists almost a century later (Helmholtz, Fechner, Wundt). Tetens' emphasis on subjective feeling and imagination did catch on, however. It strongly influenced the thinking of Fichte and Schelling and was instrumental in the growth of idealism[2], that sees the whole world as a psychological subject.

Turning consciousness into a world-system rather than a personal matter, as was the case in Hegelianism, was met with strong protest by Søren Kierkegaard in the 1840's. Working with phenomenological narratives and simultaneously attacking Hegel and what he saw as the complacency of Copenhagen society, university and church, Kierkegaard made psychological observations and reflections on personal life of unsurpassed acuity. Today he is ranked among the first existentialists and has had a tremendous worldwide impact on existential and hermeneutical psychology.

Kierkegaard's international fame is of a later date. He was first translated into English in 1930 and 1940, but his influence has always pervaded the Danish intellectual scene. Even the physicist Niels Bohr acknowledges inspiration from Kierkegaard. In formulating his principle of complementarity, that in effect says that a description of reality has to rely on two different descriptions (the electron as particle or wave) which complement each other and as such are irreducible to each other, he states a general principle which, as shown below, is also characteristic of Danish psychology.

Bohr was introduced to Kierkegaard by the philosopher Harald Høffding, who played an important role in the founding of scientific psychology at the University of Copenhagen. Professor Høffding had a keen interest in and a great knowledge of international psychology. His courses and his textbook in psychology, translated into English in 1891,[3] set the standard for generations of Danish students. Like Tetens, Høffding's aim was to reconcile empiricism and rationalism. Strongly influenced by Hume and J.S. Mill, he was a proponent of the empirical psychology, but he also insisted, Kantian-wise, upon the mind's own synthesising powers and rejected the element psychology of his time.

The laboratory in Copenhagen

On the recommendations of Høffding, Alfred Lehmann, a young engineer, was enabled to study at Wilhelm Wundt's newly-established psychophysical laboratory in Leipzig. Upon his return, and under the patronage of Høffding, Lehmann in 1886 established a similar laboratory at the University of Copenhagen, which is therefore one of the first in the world.

Formulated by Tetens in 1777, and rediscovered by Fechner in 1850, psychophysics is a method of measuring experiental change indirectly by correlating it with measurable changes in physical conditions. Demanding descriptive acumen and technical ingenuity, psychophysical investigation proved to be the right element for the philosophic engineer; but Lehmann, being of a practical bent, thought that psychology should do more. It should be of service to the society outside the laboratory. His own work on issues of work psychology and educational psychology, and his patronage of applied research, were instrumental in the very early start of applied psychology in Denmark.

When Lehmann died in 1921, he was followed by Edgar Rubin, a student of Høffding. If the founder shared the optimistic Jules Verne ethos of the early days of psychology, his successor was a product of the fraught psychological dilemmas of the 1920's. By now the major schools of psychology had been formulated and were clashing; and it seemed that the whole coherence of psychology hung in a thread. Physics, once the secure base of psychology, could no longer be counted on, having itself been entangled in unprecedented epistemological conundrums. Now physicists like Niels Bohr leaned on psychological topics in his epistemology, to the annoyance of his cousin Rubin, who decided that psychology should be left to itself until it had a clear description of its subject matter. In 1924 on his suggestion, the laboratory officially changed its name from the Psychophysical to the Psychological Laboratory.

For Rubin the subject matter of psychology was subjective experience, in particular perceptual experience. In this he was firm within the classical tradition. Neither did he doubt that subjective experience should be studied empirically. His concern was the true rendering of this experience in description. If these descriptions were not true, the data of psychology would be flawed, and so would theories built upon such material. Under his directorship the labors of the laboratory were therefore committed to the precise analysis and description of phenomenal perceptual experience under fixed experimental conditions. Until the methodology of phenomenal description was mastered, theorizing was out.

Rubin's stance had been formed while he studied under G.E. Müller in Göttingen. His investigation of figure and ground[4], carried out in Göttingen, proves how much there is to be gained from careful and precise description, and has won deserved international acclaim. During his reign a number of such studies were performed by himself and his students. In Denmark we talk about the Copenhagen School of Phenomenology, but although Rubin was acquainted with Edmund Husserl in Göttingen, this school should not be mistaken for a branch of Continental phenomenology.

Even if it shares the willingness to analyze conscious experience in every aspect, it does not share the ontological pretensions of Husserl. Similarly, the recognition of the gestalt qualities of conscious experience does not really make Danish phenomenology a brand of Gestalt psychology, since it does not share the quest for theoretical explanation of Wertheimer, Köhler, and Lewin. It is only considered to be a refinement of method, and in this it has a certain likeness to neo-positivism.

After Rubin's death in 1951 the reins were taken over by his two students and collaborators Edgar Tranekjær Rasmussen and Franz From. Both were professed phenomenologists in the Copenhagen tradition; but they had also felt cramped by Rubin's meticulous dictates and soon expanded the narrow scheme that had unneccesarily isolated Danish psychology from the contemporary issues in international psychology.

Disregarding Rubin's warnings that complex psychological phenomena could not yet be subjected to rigorous investigation, professor From published a major phenomenological analysis of the attribution of intentions to other people.[5] With this work and a series of popular essays From built a strong platform for personality psychology of the humanistic and phenomenological kind.

Against Rubin's warning that theorizing was premature, Tranekjær Rasmussen published two theoretical treatises on the foundational basis of psychology, one investigating the possibility of a scientific dynamic psychology, the other analyzing the ontology and epistemology of consciousness. In the latter attempt, Tranekjær Rasmussen was drawn to the philosophy of George Berkeley[6], which later led alienated students to a hostile identification of the Copenhagen School of Phenomenology with subjective idealism. In retrospect, however, it seems, that it was really a different message from Berkeley that the Copenhagen School taught the coming generation, and taught it well: namely, never to accept the world experienced as anything but real. The world delivered by common sense, with its abundance of forms, is the real world, and it must be investigated in its coherence and richness. This sets Danish psychology apart from main traditions of psychology that look for hidden causes behind the veil of appearances. It never accepted reductionism.

While keeping to the tenets of the phenomenological tradition, From and Tranekjær Rasmussen opened the way for theoretical discussion, even pluralism, and renewed the interest in applied psychology, which had not been a major concern under Rubin. As Tocqueville observed long ago, and as everybody knows from today's world, reform is likely to spawn revolution. In 1968 the old system was literally toppled by rebellious students, and this ushered in the present era of Copenhagen psychology. The breaking up of the old paradigm played its part in these events, but this should not be overestimated. After all, similar events took place at the same time throughout most of the Western world. In retrospect the clashes were about educational systems that were having trouble adapting to social change. Since the present era in Danish psychology is the product of these changes, this story also needs to be sketched.

The social demands on psychology

Lehmann's willingness to accept public assignments notwithstanding, for many years the efforts of the laboratory were devoted to basic research of minor practical import. Only a negligible number of people were trained, and mainly for purposes of internal recruitment. Not until 1918 was it possible to obtain a degree in psychology (Magister of psychology). By the 1940's, however, applied psychology had come to be in demand from society. In 1944 the laboratory was given the assignment of educating schoolteachers in psychology, and this led to the introduction of a general university degree in applied psychology (Candidate of psychology), which was fully implemented in 1960. The main aim of the laboratory from now on was to be the training of psychologists for public service.

Shifts in purpose and outlook are never easy to accommodate, but the magnitude of the change confronted the laboratory with staggering problems. In 25 short years – from the early 1940's to the late 1960's – the student body increased from less than 50 to more than 1000. What Rubin had felt as a strain, his successors felt as a bomb. The system was not geared to a yearly intake of several hundred students, and in the end simply caved in. This happened in 1968, when students of psychology, inspired by student unrest in other Western capitals, started a rebellion at the University of Copenhagen that led to a general university reform, in effect moving the decisive influence from full professors to associate professors, assistant professors and students. The modern era of Danish university psychology is the product of these changes, and even though the university reform of 1968 was changed in 1993, with authoritative responsibility again replacing shared responsibility, the present position of Copenhagen psychology should be understood against this background.

The era from 1968 to 1993 can be divided into two parts. The first decade was marked by an explosive growth in student intake, from a yearly intake in 1968 of approximately 200 to a yearly intake of approximately 450 ten years later, accompanied by the necessary increase of the staff to cope with the accelerating teaching load. Many graduate students were recruited as teachers to meet the demand, which was further accentuated by the fact that in 1968 a number of teachers and students from the laboratory led an exodus to the University of Aarhus where they founded the second Danish institute of psychology.

In the late 70's the growth was stemmed by governmental regulation, and the yearly intake was reduced to approximately 100 for a long period. Today it has risen to approximately 150 in Copenhagen and slightly fewer in Aarhus, but it is still strictly regulated. More than a thousand applicants are turned down each year. The restrictions have been motivated by the wish to keep down public expenditure, thus leading to budget cuts on higher education; but it has also been motivated by fear of growing unemployment among psychologists. Whereas the explosive 70's coincided with an economic boom, the austere 80's were marked by a long-drawn economic recession, with unemployment figures on a scale unprecedented in Denmark.

Even though psychologists have felt their share of the unemployment scourge, it is a notable fact that the employment of psychologists in Denmark since the war has more than doubled with every decade. From not much more than a handful in 1947, the number of psychologists in employment rose to approximately 500 in 1970, approximately 1200 in 1980, and approximately 3500 in 1990, and the labor market is still growing. This places Denmark among the nations in the world that, relative to its population, has the largest market for psychology.

The development of fields

The market profile has naturally changed over the years. The reason that the laboratory was forced to take up applied psychology in 1944 was new legislation calling for extended use of educational psychologists in the public school system. This sector was for many years the primary user of applied psychology, and grew to the extent that the education of psychologists for this purpose was moved in 1964 to The Royal Danish School of Educational Studies.

The next market to develop was clinical psychology, which was mainly in demand from the public hospital system. Slowly but steadily this market has increased fivefold from the 60's till today. This field has played a very important role in the development of applied psychology in Denmark, not so much by quantitative measure, since the sector absorbs no more than 10 percent of the country's employed psychologists, as by its public image and professionalism. As a field of research and practice it was developed at a university clinic independent of and in some opposition to the Psychological Laboratory, whose leading heads held the psychoanalytical emphasis of the clinic in disdain. In 1968, however, the clinic was amalgamated with the Psychological Laboratory as the Institute for Clinical Psychology under the professorship of Lise Østergaard. Despite some rivalry in the past, today the two institutes have a common purpose and are deeply integrated. Practical work performed with patients in a day clinic now offers students training in therapeutic methods, and these skills are in great demand not least because of a new and growing market for psychologists in private practice. Private practice has been underdeveloped in Denmark, but newly introduced official authorization of psychologists and patient eligibility for economic support through the public health service have got it moving. Since the late 80's these activities have increased fivefold.

With the addition in the 70's of a market for industrial psychology, the three classical disciplines of applied psychology were well represented in Denmark. The real growth areas of applied psychology, however, are to be found outside the public schools, in the clinic and the manufacturing plant. This has been the great educational challenge to Danish university psychology, since the new areas are ill defined as to the problems they have to solve as well as the methods they have to apply. In these areas the psychologists have to define the problems and devise the methods themselves, and prove their competence in competition with practitioners from other occupations. The reason that the Danish market for psychology has grown in the face of economic recession and rising unemployment is that Danish psychologists have proven suitable to this task.

The major new area is social work, primarily in request from municipal authorities and involving very complex and variegated problems. Today this area is by far the largest of the Danish markets for applied psychology, which is perhaps a reflection of the social problems of the recession. While 50 were occupied in this field in 1974, today the number is approaching 700.

A new, small but expanding market is health psychology, which demands that the psychologist can combine knowledge from all the classical psychological disciplines to arrive at new solutions. Another area requiring the psychologist to be a Jack of all trades, able to define problems and invent methods, is organizational psychology. It has a classical tradition, but in modern use requires great multidisciplinary competence and flexible inventiveness. This market is now expanding to an extent that makes it hard for departments of psychology to supply candidates in sufficient numbers.

Summing up, one could say that whereas the first demands on Danish psychology were to develop the traditional and well-defined fields of applied psychology, the new expansion is directed towards uses of psychology that are essential in modern society but largely undefined. The first wave of applied psychologists had to be accomplished problem-solvers; the new wave has to be problem-finders first. This offers the greatest challenge to present day researchers, teachers and students.

The objective and subjective basis for the expansion

Why is it that psychology has been so well received in Denmark and is used so extensively? There are interconnected objective and subjective reasons. Denmark has for several generations been committed to the welfare state model, supported by Social Democratic and bourgeois governments alike. This means that Denmark has a high level of public service, which – as already noted – has come to include psychological services of diverse kinds. The public service has provided applied psychology with a secure base from which it could subsequently expand into the private markets of therapy, counselling, consulting work and so on.

The objective possibilities of the welfare state go hand in hand with the more subjective psychological characteristics of Danish society which have proved conducive to the utilization of psychology. Modern Denmark is founded upon an earlier rural society of free farmers and small landowners who transformed traditional village teamwork into the co-operative movement, with shared ownership of dairies, slaughterhouses and factories for agricultural produce, that made Denmark's fortune as an agricultural exporting country. The industrialization of Denmark followed in the wake of this development, leading to small and medium-seized firms adept in niche production rather than large industries. In accord with this development, the standards of the old artisan culture were kept high, and entrepreneurs and owners were often the same. Recruited mainly from the peasantry, workers brought with them the cooperative mentality of the country. One of the consequences was that Danish workers were soon organized in Social Democratic trade unions, and to this day Denmark has probably the highest percentage of organized employees of any country in the world.

Through this development from village community to modern society a certain communal mentality has been sustained, favoring homogeneity and equality within the group, individual rights within the bounds of the common interest, social responsibility, dialogue and consensus. Everybody was to count as equal, and people overextending themselves were met with suspicion and rebuff. The ideal, in the words of the national poet and educator N.F.S. Grundtvig, coeval with Kierkegaard, was a nation "where few had too much, and fewer too little." It has been Denmark's good fortune that this Janus-faced egalitarian ideal concentrated on raising the lower end of the population towards the aspired mean, first through an immense effort of general education, championed by Grundtvig, later through social reforms propelled by the labor movement that secured the social and economic basis for the ideal. One result was the welfare state, another the democratic tradition that is deeply integrated in the Danish national character. If the first constitutes the objective basis for the expansion of psychology in Denmark, the latter constitutes the subjective basis.

Psychology requires dialogue

Despite a century of hard and ingenious work throughout the world, the subject matter of psychology has so far successfully resisted scientific attempts at objective explanation. The psychologist is still confronted with persons' sporting intentions, ideas and feelings that defy translation into causal mechanisms. The causal mechanisms discovered always seem to be just conditions for psychological functioning, and always stop short of the essential subjectivity. The human subject refuses to lie down and become a thing-like object for science to predict and control, it insists on standing up and remaining a subject.

Theoretical psychology is much chagrined by this persistence, and a standing debate has been whether one should succumb and talk to the subject in its favored language or adhere to the natural science vocabulary that we have come to identify as scientific.

Applied psychology is faced with the same conundrum, but has much less choice. To be successful, it must address people on, and in, their own terms. That is, applied psychologists must address people as subjects, equal to themselves. Dialogue, following the essential rules of reciprocity and equality, is the necessary prerequisite. The success of applied psychology therefore hinges on the success of dialogue, and this is determined not only by the competence of the psychologist but equally by the competence of the dialogue partner. The competence of the client thus becomes a decisive factor in psychological work.

Two things are here essential. The client must not view the psychologist as an expert like the mechanic or surgeon to whom you can bring your broken part for mending, but as a dialogue partner, hopefully more knowledgeable, but still an equal. The shared responsibilities of dialogue must be recognized. Secondly, in order for the cooperative effort to rise to the complexities of the problem in hand, the client must bring to the dialogue a certain level of education. People well versed in psychological thinking can make much better use of psychological services.

Both of these criteria are amply met in Denmark. Danes are well prepared for engaging in dialogue with psychologists due to the egalitarian mentality narrated above. The high and homogeneous standard of education of the population in general, including a marked attraction to psychology, makes it possible for this dialogue to take place on a progressive level. In short, it is in no little degree the competence of the Danish population that has made the successful expansion of applied psychology possible.

A plurality of views

The egalitarian mentality, with its Grundtvigian ethos that high and low should have an equal saying, accentuated by the upsurge of socialist ideology that seized students in the late 60's, played an important role in the 1968 rebellion. The university reforms that followed were designed to accommodate these ideals. At the psychological laboratory the professorial rule was toppled; but not only were high and low now to have an equal say, diverse conceptions of psychology were also to have equal representation. Within a few years the self-imposed restrictions of the Copenhagen school of phenomenology were shattered and all the major traditions and schools of psychology were introduced. Psychoanalysis, through the institute of clinical psychology; social psychology in the American style as well as in the critical German style; diverse brands of personality psychology; cognitive psychology and comparative psychology were all being introduced. It attests to the versatility of this development that even behaviorism, quite foreign to the Danish tradition and outlook, came to have a platform for a few years through the efforts of Melvin Lyon, an American Skinnerian.

Having been lost, the comforts of the reign of a single tradition now became evident. The introduction of the complete palette of psychology was also the introduction of the mind-twisting incoherence of modern psychology, where theories and methodologies talk in mutually incompatible tongues. Faced with the Babel of psychology, Copenhagen had to shoulder the legendary crisis of psychology.

Theoretical crisis added to institutional upheaval; and Copenhagen in the seventies found itself in a situation reminiscent of the classical school wars where everybody tried to take on the responsibility of order, but according to their own particular language and conception. To this was added the struggle between Marxists and non-Marxists. The pains of civil war further added to the plight since the strife took place within a single institution and between people with a common background. Precisely this background, however, made continued conflict impossible, and casualties and scars notwithstanding, the final outcome proved rather productive.

The lid neither could, nor should be put back on Pandora's box. The plurality of fields and views had come to stay. Theoretical unity remains an ultimate scientific goal, of course, but it was learnt that such unity cannot be gained by conquest, and the recognition grew that every voice has something to tell and should not be drowned. Psychology is rich, and the plurality of fields and theories is in itself an asset. Today the institute is proud of the range of psychological inquiry it sponsors, spanning from experimental investigation of visual attention[7] to anthropological field work in Polynesia[8], from the epistemological questions regarding language and psyche[9], to educational development in Russia[10].

With the recognition of diversity as a resource follows the problem of how this diversity is to be handled. How valued, but different, perhaps even incompatible, views are to be harmonized becomes not only a vital task for teaching, but also for research. In response to this, theoretical and meta-theoretical problems dealing with the foundational issues of psychology and the philosophy of science came to take high priority not only in Copenhagen but in Aarhus as well[11]. This, of course, was a return to the quest of Tetens and Høffding for theoretical alignment and synthesis, the imponderable and eternal question still being how the world of the subject can be brought into harmony with the world of natural science and the world of social science.

Theory and practice

The sudden priority of theoretical work on unsettled basic issues further changed the direction of Copenhagen psychology. The Copenhagen School of Phenomenology had established a state of what Kuhn calls normal science, that is the empirical collection of data to support and test the framework of an unquestioned paradigm. From lack of unquestioned paradigms the experimental tradition of this school consequently receded. The former profile – high in experimental work, low in theoretical work – was reversed, and this shift in emphasis distinguishes the profile of Copenhagen psychology from those usually encountered in international psychology.

This did not, however, mean an abandonment of the scientific commitment to investigate reality. The interest in theoretical psychology coincided, as already noted, with a substantial interest in the social demands placed upon the science of psychology. The interests merged, and during the 80's a novel combination of theoretical psychology and applied psychology was being forged. The continuing development of this combination of theoretical development and practical application of the theory we consider the distinctive mark and defining characteristic of contemporary psychology at the University of Copenhagen. It was arrived at via the vagaries of local history, but we believe it harbors principles of much broader importance, namely principles dealing with the relation between theory and data and between theory and practice that is relevant in nearly all scientific contexts.

Practice as empirical starting point

In the philosophy of science three primary parts of a scientific discipline are distinguished: (i) The theory, which is the total number of hypotheses and scientific concepts; (ii) The scientific data that the theory specifies as valid in testing the theoretical hypotheses; (iii) Practice, which is the application of the theory in diverse contexts, clinical, pedagogical, and so on.

At a first glance this partition seems the natural sequence of scientific progress: first hypotheses, then observations, and finally useful application. Often this proves too simple, however. The elements of science are intertwined in complex ways, and it was in response to this that Copenhagen psychology engaged in the combination that bypassed traditional experimental investigation. We think this deserves a little elaboration.

Since Karl Popper criticized positivism it has been generally accepted that scientific theories are not definable as simply a set of hypotheses. They also serve to select the sort of empirical evidence that is acceptable as data for the theory. Theory exists before data and hypotheses cannot be generated from data in the absence of a theory. Scientific theories define which data are relevant for the scientific description and, in a broader context, which methods are to be used to obtain reliable data from the part of reality that concerns the theory. To make the point rather crudely, psychoanalysis would never rely on experiments with rats, and behaviorism would never accept that symbolic interpretations of dreams have any scientific value.

Philosophical phenomenology and hermeneutics have always emphasized that sciences studying human beings as subjects must of necessity integrate a reflective element in their theories, since the subject studied is of the same nature as the describing scientist. If you make this philosophical point of departure absolute, however, you seem to be left with rather few scientific methods: introspection, interpretation, and qualitative interviews. It therefore becomes important to widen the range of scientific methods without excluding the possibility of integrating the reflective element in psychology. Let us try to look at the development in Copenhagen from this angle.

As described above, there is a difference between philosophical phenomenology and phenomenology as it was developed at the Psychological Laboratory. In its early scientific form, the object of psychology was reduced to an extent that was reminiscent of classical positivism, but even in Rubin's psychology the primary empirical method was the description of human experience. By Franz From this was extended to the intersubjectivity implicit in the "experience of other people's behavior", and by professors Martin Johansen and I.K. Moustgaard further extended to human emotions and human communication.[12]

In the 70's and 80's psychology at the University of Copenhagen displaced in a general way its empirical focus from the pure description of conscious experience to an extended concept of practice. We think this is very important. The extension goes in two directions. First, there is a displacement from the description of conscious experience alone to a combination of experience and action (experience of action). Second, there is a focusing of the elements that influence and determine conscious experience and action, since neither the conscious experience nor the action is created in a vacuum. The elements are historical in nature – social structure, institutions, socializing agents, language as a collective system and so on. The common historical paradigm was developed in different directions: in the biological evolution of the psychic and the social, the life-history perspective of the unconscious, the historical compass of the intersubjective relations. The crucial point in this displacement is that in one and the same theoretical turn it facilitates the attempt to conceive the subject's experience of her own action and the action of others, and simultaneously, in the scientific description of this, to explain why the experience is what it is, how it is determined and formed, and what is necessary to change the experience.

The central focus in most scientific programs is exactly this interchange between the subject's description of her own conscious experience and the description of the constitutive preconditions for this experience, thus avoiding the reduction of the subject's consciousness to a mere product of these conditions. The subject's own conscious reflection is defined as a parameter able to take in, and in many cases influence, the constitutive preconditions, or by the reflection itself abolish their determination.

Instead of basing psychological inquiry on a local autonomous consciousness, the conscious experience is placed in a larger setting. It is not the consciousness itself that is in focus and the conscious experience that is the empirical starting point. The empirical starting point is the interaction, the interplay and reciprocal actions between subjects. And this, of course, places the center of basic research squarely within the province of applied psychology; it is here that subjects meet, act and reciprocate. Rather than being accidental, the union of basic theoretical work and applied psychology adopted in Copenhagen is close to the very heart of psychological inquiry.

The heritage

In retrospect, psychology in Copenhagen never really veered far from the tradition. Although transformed, psychological phenomenology is still very much alive in Danish psychology. This is seen most directly in the context of personality psychology, where the tradition from Franz From is further developed,[13] and in the work of the Institute of Clinical Psychology, where, with inspiration from Kierkegaard, phenomenology is developed in the direction of existentialism. It is telling that the Institute follows the schools within psychoanalysis inspired by R. Schafer, P. Ricoeur and A. Lorenzer, which upgrade hermeneutics, rather than American schools of ego-psychology.

But also work falling outside the bounds of phenomenology proper stays within the heritage: this is clearly demonstrated by the shared commitment to an understanding of psychology that places the subject in the center and resists the reduction of subjectivity. Even within the fields most related to natural science, non-reductionism is adhered to. Danish neuropsychology under professor Rolf Willanger, for instance, has a tradition for developing the functionalistic and non-reductionistic point of view in relation to the question of cerebral localization[14]. And the Danish psychologists, who work within the tenets of the biological theory of evolution and ethology, likewise refuse to reduce the subject and its conscious experience. On the contrary, it is a key point among the biologically inspired psychologists that the property of mind is a unique and irreducible trait of animal life.

This issue

For the first issue of the yearbook three papers based on recent doctoral dissertations have been chosen. They cover the three scientific continents that psychology has to span, namely the continent of biological science, the continent of social science and the continent of humanistic science. The tectonics of these continents has traditionally caused havoc in psychology and left this science in incompatible pieces. The cry that psychology can never be a coherent science has been heard often enough. We believe, however, that the three papers disprove this sad verdict. Despite the diverse fields they cultivate, they stay on common ground. The tenets they all hold in common are precisely those that we have emphasized as particular for psychology in Copenhagen: psychology as the science of the subject, and the recognition of the irreducibility of subjective experience. We further believe that these tenets are the backbone of the true science of psychology. The papers, as well as the development of psychology in Copenhagen, proves in our mind that if this is understood, psychology needs not be sundered by diversity, but enriched.

Notes

1. L.S. Hearnshaw: *The shaping of modern psychology*, London, 1987: Routledge, p. 97.

2. Ibid. p. 103.

3. H. Høffding: *Outlines of Psychology*, London 1891.

4. E. Rubin: *Synsoplevede figurer*. København 1914. (German translation: *Visuell wahrgenommene Figuren*, 1921).

5. Franz From: *The perception of other people*. New York: Columbia University Press, 1971.

6. E.T. Rasmussen: Berkeley and modern psychology, *Brit. J. Phil. Sci.*, 1953, 4, 2-12.

7. Claus Bundesen: A theory of visual attention. *Psychological review*, vol 97, p. 523 547, 1990.

8. Rolf Kuschel: *Vengeance is their reply. Blood feuds and homicides on Bellona Islands*, Vol I-II. København: Dansk psykologisk forlag, 1988.

9. Nini Prætorius: *Subject and object. An essay on the epistemological foundation for a theory of perception*. København: Dansk psykologisk forlag, 1978.

10. Sven Mørch: Youth reproduced and investigated. Activity perspective. In: J. Ehrnroot and L. Siurala (eds.): *Construction of Youth*, p. 118-131. Helsinki, 1991.

11. See for instance Niels Engelsted, Mariane Hedegaard, Benny Karpatschof and Aksel Mortensen (eds.): *The Societal Subject*. Århus: Aarhus University Press, 1993, and Niels Engelsted, Lars Hem and Jens Mammen: *Essays in General Psychology*. Århus: Aarhus University Press, 1989.

12. I.K. Moustgaard: *Psychological Observation and Description*. Bergen: Sigma Forlag, 1990.

13. Compare the article by Erik Schultz in *The Societal Subject* op.cit.

14. Rolf Willanger: *Intellectual impairment in diffuse cerebral lesions*. København: Munksgaard 1970.

Psychoanalysis and classical tragedy

Judy Gammelgaard

It might seem a daring project to compare the course of a psychoanalysis with the course of a tragedy, motivated by the fact that the word "catharsis" is applied to the effect of each. Doesn't this imply a disregard of the great difference between a sublime form of art and a method of treatment whose aim is to relieve the neurotic patient of unbearable and life-reducing symptoms?

Furthermore, as a description of the tragedy's effect, catharsis refers to the experience of the spectator, while the word has found its place in the vocabulary of psychoanalysis as the name of a method of treatment whereby the patient is helped to abreact repressed and emotionally strong traumas.

Despite these almost insurmountable difficulties, it has proved fruitful not only for a discussion of the psychoanalytic effect, but also for the question of the foundation of experience in psychoanalytical treatment, to draw parallels to the experience of tragic art.

On the basis of my thesis (Gammelgaard, 1993), I will in the following argue for a psychoanalytic concept of catharsis which takes into consideration the characteristics of psychoanalytic treatment and shows its affinity to classical tragedy. However, by way of introduction, I would like to make a few comments on what is meant by the word tragic.

Tragic

The formulation of the word "catharsis" within what I call the dialogue between psychoanalysis and tragedy proves that the word has aesthetic as well as therapeutic meanings. This is in accordance with the tragic form of experience connecting psychoanalysis and tragedy. Nobody understood this form of experience better than *Aeschylos*, the oldest of the three great classical tragedians, when he put the following words into the mouth of his hero Agamemnon in the tragedy of the same name: Pathei Mathos: "we learn through suffering".

In his article "The Man of Flesh and Bone", Miguel De Unamuno has captured the essence of what we call the tragic sense of life with the following short anecdote: "A pedant who beheld Solon weeping for the death of a son, said to him: 'Why do you weep thus, if weeping avails nothing'"? And the sage answered him: "Precisely for that reason, because it does not avail" (De Unamuno, 1963, p. 4).

Our immediate reaction is of course to maintain that weeping does achieve something in so far as it eases our inner pressure of despair. But the deeper significance of Solon's answer ought to be equally obvious.

It is not enough that we become technically capable of curing if we don't learn how to weep.

One of the things that makes psychoanalysis a seemingly inadequate form of treatment in our modern life is its lack of limits. It insists on a perspective of infinity, and requires exhausting mental work without guaranteeing any visible or measurable results. In other words, psychoanalysis insists on a process which is time-consuming, and on a result which is part of the therapeutic process itself, in principle making this process endless. Such a temporal perspective can only with difficulty be compatible with life in a world under rapid change, demanding efficiency and visible results. In order to live up to these demands, therapists after Freud have tried to develop more effective techniques which promise relief and a better life in shorter time.

It is not least the so-called emotive techniques which are responsible for the uninspired concept of catharsis accepted into psychotherapeutic vocabulary. In simplified terms, therapeutic effect is about digging out the traumas of the past and releasing the corresponding affects.

In my thesis on catharsis I defend another definition which instead of purgation talks about clarification. I have argued that such a definition can be defended on the basis of Josef Breuer and Sigmund Freud's introduction of the cathartic method.

My thesis includes a wish to reflect and maintain the perspective of treatment in psychonalysis. Of course psychoanalysis is obligated, as mental treatment, to relieve people from unnecessary pain and suffering. But it may also result in a greater openness towards the despair which cannnot be removed. "Much will be gained", Freud said to one of his patients, "if we succeed in transforming your hysterical misery into common unhappiness" (Freud, 1893-95, p. 305).

Perhaps this does not sound very optimistic, but neither is the opposite. As in Unamuno's short story about Solon, it is not pessimism which radiates from Freud's message.

The tragic sense of life does not mean resignation but a certain kind of acceptance of the inevitable, a reconciliation to the necessary contradictions in life, or in Hegel's words "over and above mere fear and tragic sympathy we have therefore the feeling of reconciliation, which tragedy affords, in virtue of its vision of eternal justice" (Hegel, 1962, p. 51).

These words of Hegel have led me to perceive the affinity between psychoanalysis and classical tragedy. In both, a universal view of antagonism in human life is revealed and in both there is a form of reconciliation.

The drama seems to have had a special attraction for both Freud and Sophocles, and Shakespeare appears to have anticipated many of the insights Freud attained in his scientific speculations (see Green, 1979).

This affinity is not least based on the way Freud talks about mental life.

Psychic Life: Psychoanalysis

The concept of the unconscious is one of the cornerstones of Freud's theories. The unconscious was to Freud not only "une façon de parler" (Freud, 1917, p. 257), an expression which he puts into the mouth of one of his colleagues: it is dynamically active, representing in its own contradictorily free and timeless logic the repressed drives. Drives – Triebe – were to Freud more than an abstract category which can be juxtaposed or hierarchically fitted into other motivational forces. It is they that cause us to act, think and feel as we do, ant this is not willingly admitted by enlightened reason. The drives make us unwell, create disturbances in our love life and turn us into hypocrites, liars or truth fanatics (see Loewald, 1980).

Psychoanalysis deals largely with the body and the life of the body, its functions and needs, senses and feelings, its unfolding in play and dance, in delight and pain.

It is the body's representation in the psyche which demands what I have called the energetic discourse of psychoanalysis. This corresponds to Freud's definition of drives: "The concept of drive is thus one of those lying on the frontier between the psychic and the physical". (Freud, 1905, p. 168).

Of course, on one level psychoanalysis deals with meanings, interpretations and subjective motivation, but it is also about the inexpressible character of body and desire. It is in order to remind us of this – of what lies on the border between language and culture – that Freud expressed himself in energetic terms and models. In other words, psychonalysis as a science can only be understood on the basis of these two discourses, the energetic and the hermeneutic.

Had Freud not insisted on the body and its representation as a dynamic active force, he never would have been able to create his case histories or to understand dreams, jokes, the psychopathology of everyday life or the discontents of civilization. In other words, he would never have been able to create psychoanalysis as a science, characterized as essentially different from either biology or academic psychology.

In my tentative definition of a psychoanalytic concept of catharsis, it has been important for me to adhere to the above-mentioned duplicity. In my theoretical delimitation of the catharsis concept this has meant that I have studied catharsis from the point of view of metapsychology. Thus I have adhered to the economic point of view and insisted on the energetic discourse of psychoanalysis in a deliberate disagreement with one of the leading American psychoanalysts, Roy Schafer (see Schafer, 1970, 1975 and 1976).

If psychoanalysis is to maintain its scientific characteristics and agree with its object, it has to incorporate the energy discourse within a theory of meaning, as expressed by the French philosopher Paul Ricoeur (1970). This means that the psychic apparatus among other things must be understood from a quantitative point of view because, as polemically argued, a drive is not constructed as language. In other words, psychoanalysis maintains that psychic life is motivated by forces characterized by being quantity.

But does this not mean that we adopt a mechanical and deterministic point of view of the psychic realm and thus legitimize a simplified concept of catharsis, which in a psychotherapeutic perspective means to purge repressed feelings and buried childhood traumas? I don't think so.

However, the problem is solved neither by dismissing the energy concept and economic point of view of psychoanalysis nor by postulating an a priori and autonomous ego supplemented with a theory of drive neutralization. In that case psychoanalysis would become either an academically or biologically based psychology.

Catharsis in psychoanalysis

One of the most serious misunderstandings attached to the use of the catharsis concept in relation to psychotherapy is the one which makes the word analogous to emotional abreaction.

In the psychotherapeutic tradition of interpretation, reference is often made to early psychoanalytic works and to the cathartic method based on hypnosis, and the term abreaction has been established.

To make catharsis synonymous with abreaction, however, depends on a biased reading of early psychotherapeutic works. When linked to a simple understanding of recollection as reproduction of earlier experiences and a medically inspired concept of trauma, it leads to a simplified understanding of neurotic development and an equally simplified recipe for effective psychotherapy.

Neurotic people suffer from early formed and still active traumas, whose most essential elements are repressed affects. The aim of psychotherapy, which coincides with its technique, must consist in helping the patients to abreact repressed feelings and reproduce the traumatic experiences. Many therapists after Freud, from Sandor Ferenczi and his active therapy to Arthur Janov's primal therapy, base themselves on such an idea of the psychic trauma and on a purely economically founded theory of affects.

The concept of abreaction has suffered from certain ambiguities due to the fact first that the cathartic method was used with three different etiological conceptions of hysteria: the conceptions of hypnoid hysteria, of retention hysteria and of defense hysteria; and second that the concept of abreaction underwent a gradual change in accordance with the development of psychoanalytic technique and theory.

A careful reading of *Studies in Hysteria* (Freud and Breuer, 1893-95) already makes it clear that the cathartic method implied more than abreaction. To equate catharsis with this term goes in fact only for the "pure" retention hysteria. When it comes to the other two categories of hysteria, abreaction it not enough. It is necessary also to deal with the pathogenic idea. In fact, *Studies in Hysteria* is a convincing demonstration that right from the start the cathartic method consisted in helping the patient to relief through the use of words.

From my reading of *Studies in Hysteria* I have concluded that catharsis refers to the following three items: 1) the recollection of split-off ideas, which then can be made accessible for normal conscious work; 2) transformation of an emotional strong idea into a weaker by abreaction, i.e.

discharging converted affects, which again allows a more relevant handling of the corresponding idea; and finally 3) an adjustment of the split-off idea to the remaining contents of consciousness through normal work-off processes. Abreaction thus refers, strictly speaking, only to part of the process, namely what is mentioned under point 2, and cannot even here be construed as just emotional discharge. An adjustment of representation and affect also occurs (see Bibring, 1954).

Furthermore, when regarding *Studies in Hysteria* as a whole, there seems to be a certain ambiguity in Breuer and Freud's use of catharsis. On the one hand the word refers to energetic terms in the sense of abreaction, accumulation and reduction of tension. On the other hand a totally different discourse is suggested where the cathartic method, aided by language, develops a certain redemption of affect-loaded memories. Breuer and Freud talk about abreaction of repressed affects, while gradually developing a totally different discourse through the case histories fitted in between the theoretical sections. Thus a method is illustrated where the spoken word and the narrative become active means in curing. Two discourses therefore seem to converge: an energetic or economic and a hermeneutic, and the designation "catharsis" is found on the intersection of these. On the one hand catharsis refers to a purely economically defined affect discharge, on the other to the result of a process leading the affects into the associative work of thinking, in order to find a form of redemption through the narrative.

If we are to retain a psychoanalytical concept of catharsis which can be added unopposed to the method Freud gradually developed after abandoning hypnosis, the word must be linked to a series of ideas to which it was linked from the very beginning. In other words the catharsis of psychoanalytic treatment must be understood in the light of the redemption which accompanies the recollection of the psychic trauma.

The catharsis of traumatic memories

The crux of the matter in this discussion is the psychoanalytical concept *Nachträglichkeit* (in English: deferred action) which Freud introduced in "Project for a Scientific Psychology" (Freud, 1895) while presenting the story about Emma (see also *From the history of an infantile neuroses*, Freud, 1918).

Emma's phobic symptom is the result of an unconscious linking of two events separated in time. Under the impression of an experience which can be dated to adolescence, Emma interprets a similar experience which goes back several years. It is this unconscious signification that releases the repression and creates the symptom.

With the concept *Nachträglichkeit* Freud introduces a not insignificant dimension to the psychology of remembering which henceforth has the character of constructions rather than of reconstructions. However, this must not be misunderstood as meaning that Freud supposes that our stories are projections of contemporary events or misunderstandings into the past: that the last mentioned, using an expression from Jung, is to be understood as pure "Zurück-phantazieren" (see Freud, 1918). With the concept Nachträglichkeit Freud introduces a linking of past and present experiences, of reality and phantasy, which opposes a linear and causal categorization. I will show the implications of this concept by an example, not from psychopathology, but from the world of art: Freud's interpretation of a childhood memory of the great artist Leonardo da Vinci (Freud, 1910).

In this fascinating analysis Freud shows that constructed memories can have both redeeming, cathartic and creative force. The starting-point of Freud's analysis is a curious childhood memory, which appears in Leonardo's scientific notes on the flight of vultures. He remembers how a vulture came down to him in the cradle, opened the small boy's mouth and struck his lips with its tail (ibid., p. 82). This memory, Freud maintains, implies the structure of *Nachträglichkeit*, which signifies the development of childhood memories: "This is often the way in which childhood memories originate. Quite unlike conscious memories from the time of maturity they are not fixed at the moment of being experienced and afterwards repeated but are only elicited at a later stage, when childhood is already past; in the process they are altered and falsified and put into the service of later trends, so that generally speaking they cannot be sharply distinguished from phantasies" (ibid., p. 83). This idea derives from Freud's theorization from the 90's and implies that throughout life the individual rearranges past incidents and that this rearrangement may have pathogenic implications (see letter to W. Fliess 6. 12. 1896, S.E. ed. vol. 1, p. 233). However, not all incidents are rearranged in this way, only such which at the time of experience were not understood or only partly understood. The prototype of such a process is the traumatic experience, or to be more specific: the trauma is constituted in this way as a defensive action.

In his interpretation of Leonardo's phantasy, Freud permits himself to form a conclusion from analogous observations to what he knows from dreams and certain perversions. I will not concentrate on these interpretations but point out the significance of this analysis of a childhood memory for a psychoanalytical understanding of Leonardo's art.

From the interpretation of the vulture phantasy as an expression of a repressed memory of the mother's passionate kiss on the boy's lips, Freud draws the further conclusion, that in the Florentine Mona Lisa del Gioconda, Leonardo was fascinated by her smile, "for the reason that it awoke something in him which had for long lain dormant in his mind – probably an old memory. This memory was of sufficient importance for him never to get free of it when it had once been aroused; he was continually forced to give it new expression" (ibid., p. 110).

Psychoanalytic interpretation of aesthetic phenomena has often been criticized for being reductionistic. This would be a just criticism if for instance the interpretation of Mona Lisa's smile was reduced to being a repetition of the smile Leonardo kept as a memory of his mother. "It is possible", writes Freud, "that in these figures Leonardo has denied the unhappiness of his erotic life and has triumphed over it in his art, by representing the wishes of the boy infatuated with his mother as fulfilled in this blissful union of male and female natures" (Freud, 1910, p. 118).

Freud's interpretation is not to be understood as meaning that behind Mona Lisa's smile he uncovers a memory which can explain to us what Leonardo fundamentally wanted to depict. What has to be warned against is the reduction which arises when one tries to force an analysis upon the complexity of a work of art, narrowing the eye and leading the understanding back to a certain point – in this case the memory of his mother's love – which then makes the whole connection understandable. Such a procedure, which moves away from the complexity of the work of art as a whole, is as inapplicable in aesthetic analyses as in the therapeutic reconstruction process. The term *nachträglich* warns us against this reductionistic procedure. The term implies that the mother's kiss is not yet there, ready for evocation by Leonardo's brush. On the contrary, the remembrance does not exist until the moment when it is created.

The reality which might be the basis for Leonardo's Mona Lisa figure, of the kissing and caressing mother, is not present as a concrete point of reference for the analysis of the work of art. In other words, as Poul Ricoeur stated: "If the artist's brush recreates the mother's smile in the smile of Mona Lisa, it must be said that the memory of it exists nowhere else but in this smile, itself unreal, of the Gioconda, which is signified only by the presence of the colour and pattern of the painting" (Ricoeur, 1970, p. 173).

Freud may be right in his hypothesis that the smile of Mona Lisa leads us back to Leonardo's memory, but only as "a symbolizable absence that lies deep beneath Mona Lisa's smile", as Ricoeur points out (ibid., p. 174). As an absence such as this, the memory of the mother's smile does not give us any explanation of the enigma of the smile, only enhances it. In his phantasy – as in his art – there is no mention of Leonardo repeating the traumatic experience of the early and lost loved object of childhood. This exists primarily in the phantasy and the artistic creation, which therefore is more than re-creation – it is the creation of a work of art, or in other words it is both cure and symptom.

Freud's Leonardo analysis demonstrates that the traumatic memory cannot be understood as a repetition, but as a creation, not of something, it must be added, that was already there as a concrete print in the psyche. On the contrary, the elaborated memory – in this case the artistic expression – depends on the abyss existing between the I who remembering looks back and a past for ever lost, possible only to capture in a creative process. If we generalize this example it means that the concept of trauma, defined as something *nachträglich* created, does not refer to a historical event stored in the psyche and only waiting to be excavated. On the contrary, the rearrangement and transcription of psychic events both cause the repression and in the same process constitute the trauma. Generally speaking, remembering is potentially traumatic. But as shown by the Leonardo analysis, traumatization includes both pathogenic and healing elements.

Admittedly it is a long way from the catharsis of psychoanalytic therapy to the triumphant redemption of an infantile trauma which Freud interprets into Leonardo's work of art; so much so that it does not seem immediately justified to use the same term for the supposed redemption.

Nevertheless, with his Leonardo analysis Freud added a dimension to the work of remembering which made it possible, through the cathartic method, to relieve the hysterical patients of their "reminiscences" and which in much psychotherapeutic terminology has become the idea of a discharging or purging of repressed affects. However, with this analysis Freud also added the dimension of sublimation to the cathartic possibility of remembering.

With the suggestion of a psychoanalytic concept of catharsis, joining the concept of sublimation with affect-releasing, the stage is set for a dialogue with the aesthetics' catharsis, where the words "purgation" and "purification" have been the preferred translations and interpretations.

Catharsis and Tragedy

Dramatic art was born in classical tragedy, and in Aristotle's *Poetics* it found its philosophical justification. In chapter 6 of the *Poetics* Aristotle defines tragedy on the basis of the effect it is supposed to have on the audience. Here it is clearly and concisely said of tragedy, that "through pity and fear it effects relief to these and similar emotions" (Aristotle, 1982a).

Even though receptive psychological aspects are central in *Poetics'* determination of tragedy, Aristotle says very little about these if we limit ourselves to the sparse definition of tragedy from *Poetics'* chapter 6. In its entirety the definition reads as follows: "Tragedy is, then, a representation of an action that is heroic and complete and of a certain magnitude – by means of language enriched with all kinds of ornament each used separately in the different parts of the play: it represents men in action and does not use narrative and through pity and fear it effects relief to these and similar actions" (ibid., VI.7). Aristotle returns to the tragic emotions pity and fear in chapter 13, where it is said that we feel pity for a person who undeservedly falls into misfortune, and fear in relation to one who is our equal.

The fact that Aristotle has defined these essential elements of tragedy so sparsely can be interpreted in the light of an argument stated in *Politics*, where it is said, with regard to catharsis, that it will be more extensively treated in *Poetics*. Is one to understand that something has disappeared from the work that has been handed down to us? This point of view is by some considered the most plausible (House, 1958).

However, there may be another reason why Aristotle has not treated the tragedy's effect as a separate matter. This could be sought for in the nature and effect of tragedy, which for Aristotle are inextricably bound together. Perhaps we ought to abandon the idea of a relation between nature and effect entirely in order to understand that the unfolding of the tragic action in itself contains the psychic experience defined by Aristotle through the feelings of pity and fear. No matter what explanation we choose, we do not have many explicit statements from Aristotle on which to base our interpretation of the catharsis of tragedy. It is precisely this implicit definition of catharsis that has brought about such an enormous number of papers about *Poetics* and its definition of tragedy. With Gudemann we can say "that there hardly anywhere in world literature exists a passage of similar modest extent, which has brought about so enormous an amount of work" (Gudemann, 1934, p. 167).

To this ambiguity is added the grammatical ambiguity of the catharsis phrase, which in itself opens up various possibilities of interpretation (see Kommerell, 1970). In my own discussion of the tragedy's effect, Jacob Bernays' (1880) modern and medically based interpretation of the *Poetics'* catharsis has been an unavoidable starting point. For several reasons.

In my opinion, Bernays' interpretation of catharsis is the one that has formed the basis of the way the word is used in psychotherapy, and not only because Bernays introduced what he himself called a psychopathological point of view of the *Poetics'* definition of tragic effect. Personal circumstances have been important as well.

Bernays' thesis was first published in 1857 and reprinted in 1880, the same year that Josef Breuer began treating Anna O. This young hysterical woman probably inspired her doctor to talk about catharsis, in her own words calling Breuer's treatment a "talking cure" and "chimney sweeping".

Jacob Bernays was an uncle of Marta Bernays, Freud's wife. When Breuer and Freud were developing the cathartic method together, Bernay's thesis was widely known and cannot have escaped the two doctors' notice (Ellenberger, 1973; Simon, 1984).

Here I will not concentrate on Bernays' medically inspired interpretation of the *Poetics'* catharsis, nor on what might be said to be Bernays' platform, a criticism of Lessing's bourgois dramaturgy inspired by the spirit of enlightenment. I shall merely suggest that the idea of catharsis which has moved from the vocabulary of aesthetics into the vocabulary of psychotherapy probably has its roots in Bernays' medically interpreted concept of catharsis.

In my own reading of *Poetics* I have chosen two principally different accesses. I have followed Bernays', who in his interpretation subscribes to the view that fundamentally the *Poetics* is about the psychology of the audience, in particular the relief from an over-tense and painful register of feelings. With Bernays we are introduced to the idea of the effect of the tragedy as a psychosomatic process, a process bringing emotional relief.

In order to understand tragedy as defined in the first part of my article, Bernays' definition will not be sufficient. In my point of view tragedy is more than affective relief. The effect of the tragedy cannot be seen as merely therapeutic. The tragic experience implies the observation of basic psychic antagonisms, which are here experienced aesthetically. Furthermore, it is my opinion that Aristotle respects and demonstrates the supposition that tragedy has both psychological – in the sense of therapeutic – and aesthetic implications. The latter appears not least from his concise but profound analysis of the formal compositional principles of tragedy.

Therefore, Bernays' medical interpretation of Poetics must be supplemented by an interpretation or reading that emphasize these formal aspects.

I have chosen Gerald Else as a representative of an interpretation of the *Poetics* that one could call structural, because he stresses the formal and structural elements in the unfolding of tragedy, which according to Else must form the basis for our interpretation of the receptive psychological categories (Else, 1957, 1986).

In my opinion both ways of reading are necessary in order to solve the problem of how the complete and unambiguous structure, which is Aristotle's definition of the aesthetic, facilitates the unfolding of the tragic event, evoking the tragic emotions in the spectator and creating a form of catharsis which, we must assume, has aesthetic as well as therapeutic implications. I will suggest an answer to this question through a discussion of the pleasure of experiencing the tragic form of art.

Tragic pleasure

During the performance of a tragedy we are deeply moved by the hero's tragic fate, by his suffering, his death or psychological destruction, which in most cases is the result of the tragic action.

How can we understand the paradoxical pleasure which is connected with the experience of what is tragic? How explain that we can find pleasure in the performance of an Oedipus', an Antigone's or a Medea's fate – fates involving death and destruction within a kinship framework? Aristotle was absolutely confident that the family was tragedy's space par exellence. In chapter 14 of *Poetics* he suggests directly that the poet achieves the greatest possible effect by choosing subjects like murder or intentions of murder among people related by blood, as when brother kills brother, a son his father, a mother her son, or the son his mother.

Tragedy reveals things we would shrink shuddering and terrified from in real life. In the aesthetic form of dramatic art we exerience these things with a particularly intense pleasure.

It is in respect of the difference between the aesthetic form of experience and our experiences in real life that we can be justified in interpreting the *Poetic's* catharsis and its pleasure as something other than what Aristotle mentions in his *Politics*.

It has been natural to interpret the pleasure of tragedy as a result of masochism, in the sense that the pleasure of passion is a conditioned form of pleasure, depending on pain or rather on its termination (see Lipps, 1891). Although such an explanation can seem absurd it is nevertheless an interpretation of the pleasure peculiar to tragedy which is often put forward. In its most primitive form it maintains that pleasure enters when pain ceases – a passing experience of pain is a means to enhancing our mental well-being. A slightly more advanced explanation would maintain that pleasure is a form of engagement. We engage ourselves in the suffering of the hero with a particular form of pleasure.

With such a point of view one has to state that pleasure is conditioned by engagement or pity: we take on the suffering, suffer in a masochistic way. Actually in this case one cannot talk about masochism but rather the pleasure of cruelty – a pleasure which after all is a poorly hidden narcissism. Our self-esteem wins in strength through the presence of the systemic destruction of the other's greatness.

Another variety of masochistic pleasure will allow the pleasure of the suffering to be a result of the reproduction of the suffering, hence the pleasure derived from the Passion sculpture. But how can we explain that the pleasure of seeing the suffering contains a psychic pleasure? Strictly speaking, pleasure first arises when we turn away, and therefore cannot be said to have arisen through the experience itself.

We can observe the same limitation in those interpreters of the tragic who will allow pleasure to be conditional. In that case pleasure will depend on a divine principle of justice, and we leave the theatre with the pleasing feeling that punishment and reward will be distributed by merit.

But can it be said that the hero receives a well-earned punishment in tragedy? The fate of the tragic hero seems to contradict this. Obviously, Antigone does not walk to her death out of guilt. She chooses death in spite of the fact that she wishes the opposite. Oedipus' search for truth is not a punishment for transgressing what, admittedly, must be considered the greatest taboo action of our civilization: parricide and incest. Oedipus' fate is not a divinely devised punishment but a consequence of his heroic search for truth.

The pleasure of tragedy then does not depend on the termination of suffering but, on the contrary, on its presence. However, nor is it suffering as such that fills us with joy. On the contrary it reveals to us the feelings of triumphant control of pain, that we call pleasure. In other words, pleasure is not conditioned by something else but is a natural part of the tragic aesthetics' form of experience. Tragedy's effect cannot be derived from something external; and the pleasure with which we experience tragedy is not a conditioned but a natural form of pleasure, to use Aristotle's terms (Aristotle, 1982b).

Tragic suffering should not be mistaken for pessimism. Whereas a pessimistic outlook implies that life is necessarily seen as suffering, a tragic outlook implies that in suffering we see not the negation but the confirmation of life. To inflict pain on others is a negation of life. Suffering, however, is a reminder of life as a resistance to – a processing of or reaction to – destruction, pain and violence. For the same reason, tragedy, by depicting suffering, represents the victory of life over death – victory of the pleasure principle over the repetition compulsion. Thus suffering and fear are the great revelation of life. Through these we learn what life consists of and what makes it worth living.

Against this background I understand that the pleasure derived from tragic art is, in Aristotle's words, a natural pleasure and cannot be only a conditioned form of pleasure. It is not simply the pleasure of removing something painful or correcting a mistake.

But how can we differentiate between the tragic pleasure and the cathartic effect, or between the aesthetic and the therapeutic aspect of the experience related to tragic art?

It is obvious that one of the essential elements of the aesthetic experience is the natural pleasure, and that this is the true and highest goal. But does that mean that the therapeutic aspects arising out of this are merely biproducts?

This assumption would, from my point of view, imply the acceptance of the medical concept of catharsis and maintain that there is a purifying and healing effect in creating conditions for the outlet of pent-up affects. In relation to the above discussion of therapy and therapeutic effect, however, this point of view will be unacceptable. It cannot be contested that the release from intense emotions may involve psychic well-being, but this does not as a matter of course make it therapy.

If we follow Bernays and acknowledge a healing element in the effect of the tragedy, this cannot be a by- or a final product. Like tragic affects and aesthetic pleasure, catharsis is not sporadic but a process. As stated by Freud, the tragic composition opens the way to deep layers in our emotional life. How poor would it not be to see this emotional activation in itself as healing. Like tragic pleasure, catharsis is a natural and spontaneous reaction to the tragic essence.

Therefore my proposal is that catharsis cannot be compared to a purification or a cleansing, but is better interpreted by another cleaning metaphor: clarification.

Aristotle connects pleasure with the mimesis of dramatic art. It is by its reproductive or representative character in spite of the cruel things it narrates that tragedy is able to give us pleasure.

Mimesis is a basic category in Aristotle's *Poetics*, referring to art reproducing reality – not in any banal naturalistic or realistic sense but as a creative reproduction. Mimesis is a form of rendering visible which is not to be misinterpreted as a relation between copy and original.

There are several examples in *Poetics* to show that it is not a naturalistic understanding of art which underlies the idea of mimesis. Most convincing is the comparison between the poet and the historian in chapter 9. Whereas the latter narrates "what happened", the former points out "what might happen"; and "for this reason poetry is something more scientific and serious than history because poetry tends to give general truths while history gives particular facts" (Aristotle, 1982a).

That the artist is obligated to reproduce the possible but is at liberty to prefer the impossible in so far as it is probable (ibid.), shows that Aristotle puts the artistic obligation elsewhere than in relation to the immediate reality.

The poet does not present the colourful diversity of life in his art. Mimesis is not a reproduction of the surface of things, and the artist's task is not to reproduce. The mimetic representation makes something alive and actual but it does not imply that we are to look for similarities between the original and the mimetic representation. The mimesis of art is the key to understanding the pleasure it gives us.

That we can take pleasure in regarding the fate of the tragic hero at all may be based on the fact that behind the tragic events the poet produces a certain meaning and order. This is what Aristotle demands of the poetic composition: the unity and entity of time, place and action demonstrate that out of the destruction and chaos of the tragic event an impression of unity and harmony can be restored. The aesthetic form makes it possible not only to endure the painful events unfolding before us but to experience them with pleasure.

The origin of art, says Aristotle, is found in the soul of man, or to be more explicit, in two natural causes. First of all, the ability to copy is something which we can see already in the small child. Secondly, man has a spontanous joy and obtains the greatest experience in learning through mimesis. Aristotle has made mimesis a spontanous and natural force in man, containing its own pleasure, and as such it connects the child's play, dance, and artistic development. In Aristotle's arguments regarding mimesis we find again the modern psychoanalytical understanding of the play's significance for the child's ability to identify and imitate.

In play, the English psychoanalysist D.W. Winnicott says the child creates the first illusion, and in this illusion, filled with "transitional phenomena" (Winnicott, 1971), the child learns to imitate and identify. Thus the capacity for aesthetic pleasure is founded, whilst at the same time the narcissistic impotence of early childhood changes into a form of control containing a triumphant pleasure.

The child rejoices and can indefinitely repeat the game of "hide and seek" because through this he learns that things that disappear can re-appear. The triumphant feeling resulting from this can only really be understood when we realize that the experience of loss is the most fundamental and existential in human development.

The most important lesson for the small child to learn is that the loved object is neither part of nor belonging to the child but separated and out of its control. The child must learn the conditions of separation, and learn to endure the loss of unity and omnipotence. Furthermore the child must learn that the object of its love can survive the destructive and aggressive impulses the child also contains.

If fear of destruction becomes too great for the small child, the ability to work through and repair is impeded. These abilities are the basis of symbolic formation and creativity. The ability to repair is motivated by the child's wish to recreate the original experience of unity. This creation is at the same time the creation of what we call the inner life. The basis is, as suggested, that the child allows the destructive impulses to be directed against the object. By destroying the object the child can reconstruct it as part of the inner life. Loss and separation are thus the most powerful motives for any creative process.

In play the child repeats the painful experience of loss and creates with the teddybear and the doll its first illusory replacements for the inevitably lost. Later the child learns to use stories as transitional phenomena, and the child's room is populated with evil stepmothers, sleeping princesses and impotent kings. Through these transitional phenomena the child learns to replace the narcissistic violation of its own impotence with an aesthetic pleasure, helping it to endure the pain of loss and violation.

It was already clear to Aristotle that the child's play contains a mimesis, i.e. a symbolic representation, making it into much more than a simple reproduction and harmless pleasure. In play as in tragedy is repeated what was once enacted on the inner stage of psychic life. Under the protection of the aesthetic illusion we recreate and reconcile ourselves to the working remains in our unconscious of inevitable loss, violations and anxiety-filled phantasies of destruction (see Segal, 1952 and 1991).

The aesthetic pleasure of tragic art does not only consist in our identifying with the hero's fate but with the work of art as a whole, including the inner world's chaotic and destructive powers, which in the work of art receive aesthetic form.

References

Aristotle (1982a). *Poetics* (translated by W.H. Fyfe). London: Loeb classical Library XXIII.
Aristotle (1982b). *Nicomachean Ethics* (translated by H. Rackham). London: Loeb classical Library XIX.
Bernays, J. (1880). *Zwei Abhandlingen über die Aristotelische Theorie des Dramas*. Berlin.
Bibring. E. (1954). Psychoanalysis and the dynamic psychotherapies. *Journal of the American Psychoanalytic Assocation*, 2: 745-769.
De Unamo, M. (1963). The Man of flesh and bone. In: Michell & R.B. Sewall (eds.), *Tragedy: Modern essays in criticism.*
Ellenberger, H.F. (1973). *Die Entdeckung des Unbewussten, vol..1 og 2*. Bern.
Else, G. (1957). *Aristotle's Poetics: The argument*. Cambridge, Massachusets.
Else, G. (1986). *Plato and Aristotle on poetry*. Chapel Hill/ London.
Freud, S. and Breuer, J. (1893-95). Studies in hysteria. In: *Standard Edition of the Complete Psychological Works of Sigmund Freud*, vol. II. London.

Freud, S. (1895). Project for a scientific psychology. In: *Standard Edition of the Complete Psychological Works of Sigmund Freud*, vol. I. London.

Freud, S. (1905). Three essays on sexuality. In: *Standard Edition of the Complete Psychological Works of Sigmund Freud*, vol. IV. London.

Freud, S. (1910). Leonardo da Vinci and a memory of his childhood. In: *Standard Edition of the Complete Psychological Works of Sigmund Freud*, vol. XI. London.

Freud, S. (1917). Introductory lectures on psychoanalysis. In: *Standard Edition of the Complete Psychological Works of Sigmund Freud*, vol. XVI. London.

Freud, S. (1918). From the history of an infantile neurosis. In: *Standard Edition of the Complete Psychological Works of Sigmund Freud*, vol. XVII. London.

Gammelgaard, J. (1993). *Katharsis. Sjælens renselse i psykoanalyse og tragedie.* København.

Green, A. (1979). *The tragic effect.* Cambridge.

Gudemann, A. (1934). *Aristoteles: Poetik.* Berlin/Leipzig.

Hegel, G.W.F. (1962). *On Tragedy.* USA.

House, H. (1958). *Aristotle's Poetics.* London.

Kommerell, M. (1970). *Lessing und Aristoteles.* Frankfurt am Main.

Lipps, Th. (1891). *Der Streit über die Tragödie.* Hamburg/Leipzig.

Loewald, H.W. (1980). *Papers on psychoanalysis.* New Haven/London.

Ricoeur, P. (1970). *Freud and philosophy. An essay on interpretation.* New Haven.

Schafer, R. (1970). Requirements for a critique of the theory of catharsis. *Journal of Consulting and Clinical Psychology*, 35/1: 13-17.

Schafer, R. (1975). Psychoanalysis without psychodynamics. *International Journal of Psychoanalysis*, 56: 41-55.

Schafer, R. (1976). *A new language of psychoanalysis.* New Haven.

Segal, H. (1952). A psycho-analytic contribution to aesthetics. *International Journal of Psychoanalysis*, 33: 196-207.

Segal, H. (1991). *Dream phantasy and art.* London.

Simon, B. (1984). *Mind and madness in ancient Greece: The classical roots of modern psychiatry.* Ithaca.

Winnicott, D.W. (1971). *Playing and reality.* London.

Biopsychological aspects of individuation
– on the origin of and interplay between
biological individuality, personality and self

ARNE FRIEMUTH PETERSEN

Updated summary

The phenomenon of individuality constitutes a fundamental theme in psychology. In biology, however, questions related to the individual organism have been dealt with to a much lesser extent, at least until the art of organ transplantation made the medical specialists involved take the uniqueness of the individual seriously.

According to philosopher-psychologist, Gilbert Simondon (1989), evolution and development bring about periods of "metastability", where living beings may grow units or agents of control which equip them with their individual characteristics and ways of functioning. This conception of the organism as *"système d'individuation: système individuant et système s'individuant"*, which means that organisms endowed with ontogeny are born ready-made individuals but with a potential for further individuation, seems to permit a biological foundation of not only somatic individuation (mainly phylogenetic evolved *Gestalts*) but also of psycho-motor individuation (mainly ontogenetic developed *Gestalts*). "Individuation" is used here as a composite term that covers distinct types of processes which lead to the formation of different units of operation on biological, motor and psychological levels within the organism during evolution and, in some instances, after a certain ontogenetic development.

The following is a resumé of an inquiry into certain aspects of individuation advanced in a doctoral dissertation (Petersen, 1993) submitted and defended at the University of Copenhagen. As will hopefully become clear, one insight gained from this work is the primordial importance of the movement potential of organisms for the phylogeny and ontogeny of *biological individuality, personality and self consciousness* (in the sense of *"ipseity"*, i.e. an ongoing awareness of one's own activity). Animal and human movement as such do not constitute the very origin of these agents of control , but rather movement seems to have contributed – and still does contribute – to the different ways in which such control systems individuate.

1. Phenomenological distinction between personality and self

That personality and self do have different origins may already be gauged on the phenomenological level: for example, in experiments with so-called "self-confrontation" (Nielsen, 1962) where adult human subjects are confronted with films and/or sound recordings of themselves in some daily routine. In such situations, experimental subjects will typically experience a discrepancy between the filmed or sound-recorded picture of themselves and the picture which they have formed of themselves during their personal development, how they think – or believe – they appear to others.

This often dramatic experience of incongruity has been masterly described by the author and Nobel Laureate, Luigi Pirandello, in his novel *One, None and a Hundred Thousand*, 1926. What Pirandello realized was that each one of us cannot be the same person for others as we are for ourselves; that you cannot see yourself live; that your own appearance will be foreign to you while others may come to know it better than you do yourself; and that you can only see your own customary version of a body in movement, but never this Doppelganger which is known to others.

When, therefore, we are confronted with a film of ourselves, the experience of alienation may be explained as a result of the problemcharged meeting between our hypothetical or idealized conception of our own personality: our ideas about our own body-image, bearing, way of moving, speaking, gesticulating, laughing, crying, etc., as opposed to our moving body and voice viewed and recorded from a position other than our own. This dichotomy seems very close to the original situation of the ancient Greek theater, where the word *"per-sona"* arose signifying that something (the self?) is "sounding through (a mask)". "The mask" in the present context is the corporal frame. Following this classical lead, and somewhat in opposition to traditional personality theory, this expressive figure of ours is here equated with *personality*, whereas the cognitive aspects, often included in the concepts of "personality" by most personality theories, are elevated here to the control level of the self. (Further specification of personality and self are given in *Section 2* and *3(S)*, below.)

We may say that in "self-confrontation situations" *we observe our personality "through the spectacles" of our self* : through the ideas about our own expressive figure and its body-language which we have formed more or less consciously from childhood onwards. This is no doubt why most people are nearly shocked when AV-recordings of themselves are played back to them for the first time. Inspired by such phenomenological reports, personality may be said to be a non-cognitive entity – *a pure psycho-motor phenomenon;* i.e., a result of motor coordination which the owner of the personality may come to know only partially.

This does not apply to the self (in the Socratic sense of *"heauton"*). Although everyone's *self-system* as a whole cannot directly be observed by its owner or by others, as William James thought (1890, p. 400), we do nevertheless constantly have a sort of "symptomatic" experience of our self – a running report about how things are going relative to what we expect and have planned. Judging from the way in which other people pursue their aims and work, make decisions, weigh their words, etc., we may infer that they too are in possession of such a steering agent – *the self as a pilot of the human organism* as Plato already so strikingly conceptualized it.

We may conjecture that the self, considered as the control agent of long-term planning, arises in tempo with the child's growing understanding of his position in the family and its surroundings. He may himself govern some part of his own behaviour and make plans for future occupations. Following K.R. Popper (1976, p. 190) and S. Epstein (1973, p. 407), we may consider the human self to be a feed-back result of theory-making, especially theory-making about the person himself; i.e., the use he wants to make of himself in life.

Together with the biopsychological evidence given below, these phenomenological indications are taken as a *prima facie* reason to distinguish between personality and self. The distinction corresponds to the commonly cherished idea that personality expresses itself through *the manner* in which a person speaks or writes, while the self, or the ego, can only be gauged from *what* the person says – from *the content* of his utterances. Obviously, personality and self interact intimately, indeed often as closely as in the cases of speech and handwriting.

2. Tentative distinction between biological individuality and personality

Multicellular organisms maintain their life functions by means of a great number of control systems at different levels of organization. Viewed in relation to the nervous system, these levels seem to be arranged hierarchically, with the phylogenetically oldest control systems at the base and the phylogenetically youngest at the top of the hierarchy. The distinguishing characteristics of these different agents of control are *their differences in control function*, two of which will be specified in the following paragraphs under the headings, "biological individuality" and "personality" (the latter viewed here as the result of motor control).

The phenomenon of *biological individuality* refers to the generally acknowledged evidence that in each individual there occur individually specific biochemical processes. A first criterion of biological individuality rests on the immunological law which states that foreign tissue grafted onto an adult individual of the same mammalian species will be rejected as a result of the formation of antibodies directed against antigens in the transplanted tissue.

The existence of the specific "individuality differentials" has consequences for large areas of the life sciences. According to the medical biologist R.J. Williams (1956, pp. 177f.), biological individuality has been demonstrated to be particularly important in the following areas: (i) the formation and growth of bone, muscles, skin and circulatory systems, as well as in the composition of tissue, lymph, blood, cerebrospinal fluid, urine, etc.; (ii) enzyme functions in tissue, blood and other body fluids; (iii) pharmacological reactions to many drugs such as morphine, nicotine, caffeine, alcohol and various carcinogens; (iv) quantitatively different requirements for various specific nutrients such as minerals, amino acids, vitamins and others; (v) differences in taste and smell responses and tolerances to heat and cold stimulations.

There are thus grounds for assuming that the varying susceptibility displayed by individuals to physical and mental diseases has its roots in individual variations regarding biological constitution, although environmental influences are often required for the disease to be released. Similarly, there are also reasons to expect that many individually specific patterns of behaviour arise from *quantitative* differences between individuals with respect to requirements for nutrients, liquids, mobility, rest, sleep etc. Knowledge about biological individuality may therefore be an important branch of the study of behaviour and of personality when we wish to determine how individual variability and environmental variability interact in behaviour and personality.

In contradistinction to personality, the biological individuality of an organism may, in principle, be determined from the *metabolisttypes* and *genotypes* alone, although such determinations are difficult to carry out *stricto sensu*. One reason for this is the number of genes and their possible combinations. Another reason, which will be further elaborated below, is that not all characteristics of an organism are due to gene action but rather to differences in metabolic chemistry. This kind of individuation may, from early on, have had the function of preventing invasion by foreign organisms thus contributing to the evolution of distinct individuals in the animal kingdom.

As emphasized by Peter Medawar in his work, *The Uniqueness of the Individual* (1981, p.134), it is in the *combination* of hereditary factors, not the factors themselves, that we find the source of the biological uniqueness of the individual. "One individual differs from all others not because he has unique endowments but because he has a unique *combination* of endowments. The number of hereditary factors from which these combinations can be built up, though large, is finite, but the combinations themselves are more numerous than the individuals who can enjoy them, so that for each man actually on stage there are hundreds of possible men still waiting for a cue behind the scenes."

The phenomenon of *personality* may be viewed as the result of an interaction between, on the one hand, the *dispositions to act* which are inherent in the biological individuality and, on the other hand, the *behavioural patterns and skills* related to the execution of these dispositions. According to the logic of problem-solving analyzed by Popper (1966), behavioural patterns and skills originate as acts of trial and error-elimination. Their automatization is thought to be controlled from the cerebellum (Marr, 1969), a process that leads to simplifications of the motor part of the tentatively corroborated solutions to problems.

It is the result of a total integration of such automated acts of problem-solving that is equated here with the personality of an individual; i.e., those aspects of the organism – animal or human – which others recognize as "corporal language", "expressive and gestural communication", attitude, bearing and so on. In the case of Man, these aspects are often referred to as "personal habits and style". Identification between individuals in higher mammalian species has turned out to take place in a similar way. In some respects a dog can have just as well-marked a personality as his master, a fact that will not surprise dog-lovers. But what about the personality of *Drosophila melanogaster*, the fruit fly?! Indeed, it can be argued that all species which go through ontogenetic development may allow individual-specific problem-solving and thereby the formation of individual-specific motor patterns which members of the given species take to be personal identifiers of any particular individual among themselves.

Accordingly, personality can only be determined by examining the *phenotype* of the individual, including his behavioural patterns (often referred to by the dubious term, "habit"). The period in which *behavioural* novelties are most likely to occur is during childhood, and the longer this period tends to be for the species concerned, the more behavioural novelties there will be. Improvisation and play behaviour have proved to be very important in the development of the individual, all the more so in the case of juveniles receiving only a minimum of "instruction" from the adults around them. As pointed out by Jerome Bruner (1976), Man seems to have settled for the longest childhood in the animal kingdom. No wonder, perhaps, that we find here the greatest behavioural experimentation coinciding with the occurrence of the most highly-developed personalities among living beings.

What conspecifics can identify and react to in each other may be assumed to be a resultant of, or a kind of "epi-phenomenon" to, each individual's ontogeny of behavioural acquisition. Shakespeare depicts the drama of recognition in several scenes of his plays where even close friends fail at first to *identify* each other after years of separation, although facial lineaments and stature give them an immediate experience of "something familiar", of *recognition*. A particular stance or gesture may, according to Shakespeare, be enough to make *identification* possible later on.

Not all of what constitutes personality is at the subconscious level for the individual in question. We all have "an idea of" and "a memory of" our own personality. We are, however, not much aware of our personality and how we influence other people in the same direct way as we are aware of our self. Regarding the individuation of personality, Popper and Eccles (1977, pp. 472f.) remark that "...personality is itself partly the product of actions done in the past. To a certain degree the personality somehow really does form itself actively. Admittedly, it may be partly pre-formed by its genetics. But I think ... that a great part of the formation is really achieved by the free actions of the person himself ... Now this is an important but very difficult idea. Perhaps one could try to understand it if one thinks that the brain is actually partly formed by these actions of the personality and the self." This corresponds to Karl Duncker's (1945, p. 13) equally pertinent remark concerning problem solving and personality: personality or "character, so far as it is shaped by living, is of the type of a resultant solution... to innumerable problems, great and small."

Within the individual person, we may consider personality as "the *conservative* power", since one of its roots, the biological individuality differential, is transmitted by *genetic instruction*. To use Popper's terminology, *personality* is the "unproblematic background" on which "the *revolutionary* powers" of the *self* may sometimes carry out its *selective acts*, thereby adding new aspects to the personality – new skills, new gestures, new movements, etc. It is by means of this whole *behaviour potential*, this "behavioural individuality", that the individual (whether animal or human) can maintain its special organic equilibrium with the environment. This equilibrium will be differently organized from individual to individual, partly because the biological individualities are different due to quantitative differences in species-typical "needs" and "drives" that determine the intensity and duration with which certain behaviours are performed, and partly because the experiences and skills of every individual become different during the process of problem-solving which is required in order to establish the balance with the immediate environment.

3. Individuation through differentiation and integration

Interpreting Simondon's *"système d'individuation"* we may say that, seen from our point in time, evolution has already led to the establishment of a huge number of species populated by individuals. In most multicellular species, however, where the individuals run through an ontogenetic development, not all features of the individual are individuated at birth. To come to expression, the responsible hereditary endowments have, so to speak, to channel their effects through developmental processes, which are open to environmental influences to varying extent and at varying times.

In order to trace the phylogeny and ontogeny of biological individuality, personality and self, reference is made below to a number of recent life-science results (others' and my own) which corroborate the distinctions outlined in *Section 1 and 2*.

The ensuing experimentally based arguments lend support to the view that (I) the biochemically monitored biological individuality began as primitive chemical cycles, that (P) the motor-controlled behavioural *Gestalt* or *personality* ("persona") is the ontogenetic result of an interaction between individual-specific dispositions to act and problem-solving strategies adopted and learned by the individual, and that (S) humans actively construct their *self-system* ("*autos*") upon the edifice of a phylogenetically much older *animal consciousness* or self-surveyor system ("*ipseity*") supposedly shared by all mobile organisms.

(I) On the origin of biological individuality.
Following recent progress in molecular biochemistry and evolution mainly due to the work of the German biologist, Günther Wächtershäuser, a new picture is emerging of how the first individuated organisms may have arisen. This is a most promising view on the origin of life which attempts to explain what the unsatisfactory "primordial-soup" theory never really managed to do.

Wächtershäuser's (1988) main thesis is that the first organism-like creatures on Earth were surface-bound chemical cycles which constitute the *first* of three major stages of organic evolution: "Organisms at this *early stage* of evolution were drastically different from anything we know. These organisms were acellular and lacked a mechanism for division, but they could grow. They had neither enzymes nor a mechanism for translation, but they did have an autocatalytic metabolism. They had neither nucleic acids nor any other template, but they possessed inheritance and selection. Although they could barely be called living, they had a capacity for evolution ... life at this earliest stage consisted of autocatalytic, chemical reactions confined to an essentially two-dimensional monomolecular organic layer. These surface organisms (surface metabolists) were anionically bonded to positively charged surfaces (e.g., pyrite) at the interface of hot water."

At the *second stage* of evolution arose more complex, semi-cellular organisms which were equipped with surface-bound membranes, nucleic acids, and enzymes. Of particular relevance for our discussion of individuality is the description of how membranes evolved: Chemically, membranes can have evolved as a bi-product of the surface metabolists' production of primitive lipide-molecules, which gradually came to cover the metabolists themselves – a decisive step, which Wächtershäuser (op.cit., p. 462) characterizes as *"the first instance of individuation"*.

Thanks to this development, regulation of isolated biochemical cycles became advantageous which led to the "invention" of enzyme-control of the metabolic processes and, later, to the evolution of genetic coded enzymes. Wächtershäuser (op.cit., p. 460) says: "Cellular evolution ... consists of a genomic evolution of sequences grafted onto an older and primary evolution of unfolding biochemical pathways ..." This means that genes and gene-control of organic characteristics only came into evolution a long time after the surface metabolists had established themselves as primitive individuals (a state of affairs which may elucidate undecided questions of present-day genetics). Evolution at this stage may be considered as the breeding-ground for all the basic features with which we are familiar in the existing cellular forms of life. The genetic machinery, enzymes, membrane pumps and electron transport chains were all in place before cells without mineral support arose.

At the *third stage* real cellular organisms arose by lifting themselves free of the supporting substratum and, thanks to increasing mobility, began conquering larger and larger parts of the globe. Some of them simultaneously developed greater individual autonomy and more complex biological individualities. Wächtershäuser (op.cit., p. 463f.) proposes two ways in which such cellular individuation may have taken place: (a)"Abstriction", where semi-cellular membrane lipid-molecules formed a loop-structure, which may then have been tied off (ligated) from the supporting mineral; or (b) "Mineral-inclusion", where semi-cellular membranes obtained mineral support by encircling a mineral grain which later was either expelled from the now spherical cell or stayed within the cell, taking part in the chemical life there. For Wächtershäuser, genuine cell formation is the first step towards *speciation* since a distinction between organism and environment can only be drawn when organisms are closed up as in the case of membrane closed cells. From that moment *ecological relations* also begin to exist, and the legacy of this third stage of evolution is still with us in such phenomena as competition and symbiosis between species, predation, parasitism, etc.

What may this "molecular genesis" add to the picture of biological individuality which was sketched in *Section 2* above? First, it can be noted that apparently one of Nature's first dispositions was to give rise to discrete individuals. To start with, the biochemical individualities of the lower organisms cannot have been very pronounced, and the differences between them were of little biological importance. With the evolution of protozoa and metazoa living in different habitats, however, natural selection brought about animal species, whose members possessed biological individualities of increasing biochemical complexity and difference – until the point was reached in mammals, where every individual became distinct and unique. Even identical twins never became alike in all aspects.

(P) *On the origin of personality ("persona")*
Thus having specified personality as a mainly psycho-motor product of problem solving (summarized in *Sections 1 & 2*, above) a number of observations on small children have been made as to how (A) *preprogrammed, expressive behaviour* and (B) *acquired motor skills* may become characteristic features of the individual who carries them out, even as the involved operations solve concrete problems for the child.

(A') The result of this preliminary test of the above hypothesis of personality tends to show that *expressive behaviour* such as posture, stance and walking develop according to preprogrammed sequences of movement patterns which are both typical for our species and typical for the individual child. This is clearly seen in children who are not forced to sit, stand and walk before they themselves take the initiative which, unfortunately, is not the normal situation. A boy, aged 7-13 months, who was allowed to follow the rhythm of his own development, was systematically observed during the period when he came to master upright walking. These observations showed, (i) that walking is the outcome of interactions between factors of anatomy, tone, general maturity and previous motor development; (ii) that walking is achieved through the child's conscious use of "slow-motion" when a new position or movement is tried out for the first time, followed by a period of rhythmical repetitions of the new elements; (iii) that the aspect of "repetition" is also apparent in the various forms of motoric play (it seems to be a very efficient method for the child to "play away" non-economic ways of moving through a process of selective elimination); (iv) that a child who has been allowed to pursue his motor development at his own tempo, grows up with a greater confidence in himself and with a better knowledge of the limits of his own capabilities than children who are "helped" too much through (ambitious) instructions from parents; and therefore (v) that the personality development of most children, such as it may come to expression in their different ways of walking, to a large extent will be the (labile) result of too much instruction from outside.

(B') The acquisition of motor skills was observed in two small boys aged respectively 18-22 months and 17-28 months, who, during these periods, learned the basic operations in "Lego"-construction and how to drink from a cup. These observations showed, (i) that the child's motivation for solving these manipulatory problems is essential for learning the involved movement patterns for which there are no preprogrammations as such; (ii) that playful "repetition" of skilled movements is more efficient than adult-induced "repetition" since children most often are more motivated for play than for imitation; (iii) that acquired skills seem to be more under the influence of how others carry them out than is expressive behaviour, which may be due to situational differences of acquisition.

Taken together with evidence from research on the relationships between personality and tone as well as on phantom limbs and their movement, these observations lend support to the view that personality develops in tempo with the unfolding of inborn movement potentials and the acquisition of new skills, for which there is no, or limited, preprogrammation. Personality development thus presupposes an ontogenetic development during which physiological calibration of all mastered movements will normally lead to an individuation of personality into the unique *Gestalt*, by means of which the individual may be recognized by others. Finally it is argued that animals too possess personality to a varying degree, depending on how much freedom of choice their ontogenetic development allows for acquiring individually specific behaviour patterns and skills.

(S) On the origin of the animal self ("ipseity") and the human self ("autos")
In trying to test the hypothesis of the human self described above, it is first argued that the development of self presupposes that the person possesses an individuated consciousness. This implies that his or her *conscious* and *unconscious* representations and expectations of the world appear to the person as something coherent and belonging to him or her. Viewed in an evolutionary perspective, consciousness may have started to evolve after *stage 3*, mentioned in *Section 3(I)* above, when sucessors of the first organisms began to move around. Perhaps evolution simply favoured a magnification and storage of the so-called "efference copy" (von Holst, 1954) analogous to the exaggeration of the nerve impulses found in electric fishes. In any case, the evolution of a conscious representation of a changing world may be considered as *a solution to the problem of movement*. One important function of an individuated consciousness would then have

been – and may still be – to represent a world of change for the moving organism. Consciousness at these early stages may have functioned as a tool of navigation and a primitive spatial memory ("cognitive map"). For such reasons it may be conjectured that animals have consciousness, while plants have not. As a next step, reflexive consciousness began to evolve in higher mammals (such as the *canis* family) and primates (such as the chimpanzee). In a following step, development of the human self then began when individual planning of action, more or less independent of species-typical behavioural releasers, became a possibility.

Based on the assumption that the human self develops as a feed-back product of theory-making, especially by theorizing verbally about oneself and one's relationships to others, a number of observations and tests were carried out on small populations of normal children and autistic children, who had neither much language nor any other means of communication (Petersen, 1989a).

1° – Observations of the development of language expressions in autistic children were compared to counts of language expressions (words, utterances, signs, etc.) in a standard population of normal children (Capute et al., 1986). The comparison showed marked deficits in autistic children's capacity for using language and other communicative means. Only 2 out of 12 randomly selected autistic children approached the level of normal development of language expression which indicates that most autistic children do not possess any means for making explicit their expectations and theories about the world and themselves. Perhaps for that reason, they are incapable of forming a self-concept.

2° – A study was carried out on the possible correlation between language problems in 4-year-old children and their difficulty of perceiving affects in other children of the same age. Forty-six children selected from nursery schools were tested individually with Helen Borke's (1971 & 1973) "Interpersonal Awareness Test", after having passed Dr. Chevrie-Muller's (1986) screening test for language impairment. The result showed that 26 children scored normally in the screening test, while 20 children showed mild (11) to serious (9) troubles with language. The results of the Borke-test was that 15 children failed, and 30 children passed the test, while 1 child was left out. A comparison of the two tests showed that 12 out of the 15 children, who failed the Borke-test, also had some kind of language problem. Of the 30 children who passed the Borke-test, only 8 had problems with language. This result is statistically significant at the *level of 0.001*, which means that it is not excluded that there is a connection between having "problems with language" and "problems with recognizing affects in others" during child development. Seen in relation to what is known about the autistic child's blindness to other people's feelings, expressions and non-verbal communication (Hobson, 1987), the present result of normal children may indicate that even minor deficits in language performance may make themselves felt in the conative domain.

3° – A study of space-time orientation in autistic children was carried out with the help of video-recordings made in a specially equipped play room with one child at a time accompanied by an adult known to the child. The same 12 children, as in 1°, participated individually here. Different tasks were recorded in half hour sessions. For example, the adult asked the child to find a toy which the child, showing little interest, had abandoned 5-10 minutes earlier. A request such as "Give me the skittle!" would be accompanied by movements and signs encouraging the child to start to look for the wanted object. It turned out that 5 children did not seem to understand the request. Of the 7 children who actually showed signs of understanding the demand, only 2 managed to localize the "uninteresting" toy. These two children were also the ones who spoke the most among the children of the group. When compared to general observations of autistic children, these results do not contradict the interpretation that autists do not seem to have developed cognitive functions that can deal fully with abstract space-time relations – functions which here are conjectured to develop simultaneously with language performance.

4° – An observational study was made in order to get an impression of the autistic child's capacity for pursuing plans of action and for taking part in common activities – items which are essential for the specification of the self summarized above in *Section 2*. It was assumed that by taking part in a joint activity the child would reveal his self, as partners in common activities normally do, by the way in which he would exchange looks with his partner (the so-called "cooperative glance", according to Petersen & Ahlmann, 1991).

The experimental group of autistic children was the same as before. A group of 12 nursery school children, aged 3-5 years, constituted the control group. Video-recordings of the experimental group, similar to those used in the preceeding studies, were analyzed where situations with joint action between child and adult occurred (e.g., doing a puzzle, making a drawing, manipulating objects). Video-recordings of the experimental group were similarly analyzed.

Before summarizing the results of this possible test of self-development, a few words have to be said about cooperative looking in the control group. The children of this group accompanied their activities with frequent glances when starting up a new activity and when enjoying a joint activity that had got underway. In these situations, activities which were not too complicated to perform seemed to be well-synchronized with about 10 short glances per minute (the duration of the longest glance was about 4 seconds). In situations where a joint activity was accompanied by agonistic tendencies, the glance frequency was about 7 per minute, and the longest glance lasted about 8 seconds. In cases where the activity itself became too difficult or absorbing for the children, both frequency and duration of the glances decreased. As will appear from the following observations of interactive glances in autistic children, similar patterns were not to be found. Indeed, they seem to avoid interactive glances as much as possible. As is the case with the neurotic child, this *strategy of not-looking-at-others* is here taken to be an expression of the child's central propensity structure: the self considered as activity planner and collaborating problem-solver.

The results of counts and measurement of interactive looking by members of the experimental group divided them into three sub-groups : (i) 7 out of 12 autistic children, some 58%, did not use much communication by looking during their joint activity with the adult. It was noted that 3 of those 7 children glanced accidentally a few times at the adult. According to the chosen criterion, none of these children can therefore be said to have developed a proper self-concept at the time of testing. (ii) 4 of the 12 autistic children, about 33%, made some communication by looking at the adult while carrying out joint action with her. In this case there was on average 1 glance per minute among these children. Judging from the manner in which these 4 children solved the proposed tasks and interacted with the adult, their self-development was considered to have begun. (iii) The remaining 1 child of the experimental group was the only one who showed any normal communication through looking during interactions with another person. Furthermore, he often asked how the various parts of a task should be carried out. Since these observations also are in accordance with available information about the general development of this child, it may be justified to infer that he had managed to establish the main basis for normal development of self. Nonverbal communication with the child and intensive language-intervention were some of the means used by the child's family in an attempt to contribute to this surprising development. The author presumes that these efforts have had an effect.

Although this study was carried out on relatively small samples, the results suggest that active communication helps the child to grasp regularities in the outside world and to form theories about them. Minor language deficits in normal children and serious communication deficits in autistic children influence this process in ways that may hamper the normal child's appreciation of emotional expressions in others and invalidate the autistic child's basic space-time orientation as well as his development of a proper self.

The results are not conclusive as they stand but, compared to similar data and interpreted in the light of recent theories on development of the mind in early childhood, they may, nevertheless, lend support to the view that the self arises through intimate interaction with others right from the start, and that language functions are crucial if the growing person is to succeed in developing his own pilot to guide him through life.

4. In conclusion

The fundamental problem of any science of personality and of self, the difficulty of discovering *invariants* in a field where variation may be even more pronounced than in the domain of biological individuality, has been met in the work, summarized here, with a theory of hierarchical control systems of a bio-psychological nature. Personality and self are viewed, in agreement with H. Wallon (1938, pp. 153-154), as functionally distinct systems of control organized in hierarchy with other control systems which contribute to the formation of the individual as a harmonious totality.

The individuation of three such agents of control – biological individuality, personality (*"persona"*), and self (*"autos"*) is outlined, and it is shown that the first two formations (the biochemical control of individuality and the motor control of personality) resemble control systems found in the animal kingdom. The third and last-mentioned formation, described here as the self-surveyor system of the organism, a continuous awareness of one's own activity (*"ipseity"*), is thought to exist in single individuals of all mobile animal species. The self, considered as the steering agent for long-term planning (*"autos"*), may only develop fully in Homo sapiens, assuming that it should turn out that higher cognitive and language functions are necessary for this type of individuation process to occur.

Furthermore, it is argued that this Socratic self arises as a feedback product from theory-construction, and that the contents of the human self typically are centred on the individual's personal life-plans.

Inspired by recent molecular-biological dicoveries of surface-metabolic proto-organisms, the phylogneny of consciousness (*"ipseity"*) is traced back to the mobile successors of the surface metabolists. It is speculated that consciousness at this early stage may have functioned as a tool of navigation and as a primitive memory ("cognitive map"), and that this may still be the core functions of consciousness in more evolved, contemporary species. An unequivocal representation of the organism's environment, relative to its own activities and whereabouts, is further taken to be a necessary condition for the later appearance of the human self-system (*"autos"*). On the basis of my own research, it is claimed that patterns of automatized body movements and coordinated movements involved in presemantic or nonverbal communication constitute what others may recognize as the personality (*"persona"*) of the individual animal or human being. This also has consequences on the level of activities, where the distinction between *personalized behaviour* and *autoregulated action* accentuates the need for a general distinction between *behaviour* and *action* (as introduced in Petersen, 1989b).

Personality and self are conjectured to be two different individuating systems, where the personality seems to individuate mainly through *upward causation* from the phylogenetically older level of biological individuality, while the Socratic self seems to individuate mainly through *downward causation* from the phylogenetically younger level of language and thought products. A hypothesis about the necessity of active symbol communication for the normal ontogeny of the human self is then put to test, preliminarily with a group of children showing various language problems and a group of autistic children with little or no language. The ensuing results do not contradict the hypothesis. Until something else has been established, it may be held that early socio-affective interaction and communication with others are essential for the child's construction of theories about the world and himself.

Apart from contributing new testable theories of personality, self and autism (the apparent ontogenetic counterpart to the normal self in the sense of *"autos"*), the present analyses render the *concept of identity* obsolete by implying that concepts such as "personal", "ethnic" or "cultural identity" rest on untenable foundations. Existence of a logico-mathematical concept identity cannot, strictly speaking, be found in any part of the living world – be it the somatic, the psychic or the social domains.

References

Borke, H. (1971) "Interpersonal Perception of Young Children: Ego-centrism or Empathy?", *Developmental Psychology*, vol. 5, pp. 263-269.
Borke, H. (1973) "The Development of Empathy in Chinese and American Children Between 3 and 6 Years of Age: a Cross-Culture Study", *Developmental Psychology*, vol. 9, pp. 102-108.
Bruner, J. (1976) Introduction to *Play*, Ed. J.S. Bruner *et al.*, New York: Penguin Books.
Capute, A.J. et al. (1986) "Clinical Linguistic and Auditory Milestone Scale: Prediction of Cognition in Infancy", *Developmental Medicine and Child Neurology*, vol. 28, pp. 762-771.
Chevrie-Muller, C. (1986) "Evaluation des aptitudes psycho-linguistiques de l'enfant (3-4 ans)", *1er Colloque CNAMTS-INSERM*, vol. 144, pp. 537-552.
Duncker, K. (1945) "On Problem-Solving", *Psychological Monographs* vol. 58, N° 5, pp. 1-112.
Epstein, S. (1973) "The Self-Concept Revisited; Or a Theory of a Theory", *American Psychologists*, vol. 28, pp. 404-416.
Hobson, R.P. (1987) "Beyond cognition: a theory of autism", in Dawson, G. (Ed.) *Autism: Nature, Diagnosis, and Treatment*, New York: Guilford, pp. 22-48.
James, W. (1890; 1950) *Principles of Psychology*, New York: Dover Publications, vol. 1.
Marr, D. (1969) "A theory of cerebellar cortex", *Journal of Physiology* (London), vol. 202, pp. 437-470.
Medawar, P. (1957; 1981) *The Uniqueness of the Individual*, 2nd Edition, New York: Dover Publications.
Nielsen, G. (1962) *Studies in Self Confrontation*, Copenhagen: Munksgaard.
Petersen, A.F. (1989 a) "Théorie et observations relatives au développement précoce et à la pathologie du soi", *Les Cahiers du Cerfee*, Montpellier: Université Paul Valéry, vol. 2, 1990, pp. 118-158.
Petersen, A.F. (1989b) "Vers une théorie du comportement", in Leroy, C. (Ed.) *Compor-tement et Communication*, New York: Medsi/McGraw-Hill, pp. 15-30.

Petersen, A.F. (1993) *Træk af individuationens biopsykologi*, Copenhagen: Museum Tusculanum Press, pp. 1-175.

Petersen, A.F. & Ahlmann, L. (1991) "Aspects du regard interactif chez le jeune enfant", *Les Cahiers du Cerfee*, vol. 5, pp. 161-171.

Pirandello, L. (1926; 1933) *One, None and a Hundred Thousand*, Translated by Samuel Putnam; New York: Dutton.

Popper, K.R. (1966) "Of Clouds and Clocks: An Approach to the Problem of Rationality and the Freedom of Man", *The Arthur Holly Compton Memorial Lecture*, 1965, St Louis, Miss.: Washington University Press, pp. 1-38.

Popper, K.R. (1976) *Unended Quest*, Glasgow: Fontana/Collins.

Popper, K.R. & Eccles, J.C. (1977) *The Self and Its Brain – An Argument for Interactionism*, New York-Berlin: Springer-International.

Simondon, G. (1958; 1989) *L'Individuation psychique et colective*, Paris: Editions Aubier.

von Holst, E. (1954) "Relations Between the Central Nervous System and the Peripheral Organs", *The British Journal of Animal Behaviour*, vol. 2, pp. 89-94.

Wallon, H. (1938; 1982) *La Vie Mentale*, Paris: Edition Sociales.

Williams, R.J. (1956) *Biochemical Individuality: The Basis for the Genotrophic Concept*, New York: John Wiley.

Wächtershäuser, G. (1988) "Before Enzymes and Templates: Theory of Surface Metabolism", *Microbiological Reviews*, vol. 52, pp. 452-484.

Personal locations and perspectives
– Psychological aspects of social practice[1]

OLE DREIER

I have been asked to give a brief presentation of the argument of my recent book (Dreier, 1993). It is a study of a particular area of social practice: the psycho-social practice of psychological therapy and counselling. Prevailing notions about the relationship between theory and practice and about professional expertise are problematic. Hence it can come as no surprise that the construction of analytic tools suitable for grounding and developing current practice is often neglected. All too often, the relevant literature is narrowed down, so as to present only a collection of examples surrounded by sketchy notions. This state of affairs has devastating consequences for our reflection on and development of practice. In order to be able to reconsider and develop our practice in a collaborative and thorough way, we must have an appropriate multilayered conceptual framework at our disposal. Therefore, my primary aim is an analytic one: to develop a set of concepts, a suitable theoretical frame of analysis.

The particular conceptual approach I have elaborated is based on the fundamental work of "critical psychology" (Holzkamp, 1983). It has served as my analytic means to uncover problems and possibilities in current practice and has also paved the way to introduce more specific and concrete concepts about this particular practice. Moreover, my analytic approach is intended to be relevant for the study of problems and possibilities in other areas of practice as well.

It is difficult to present so wide-ranging a topic within the boundaries of a paper. Those interested may consult the English summary in my book (ibid., 309-350). It is divided into nine chapters each of which examines a particular aspect of psycho-social practice from a particular perspective. Analytic concepts are introduced and elaborated when needed along the way. Therefore, I have decided to focus this paper on the basic framework

---

[1] I would like to thank Jean Lave for constructive comments on an earlier version of this article and for numerous inspiring discussions on its issues and standpoints.

I developed and applied. In the end, I shall briefly indicate what kind of analysis of psycho-social practice it is geared to open up.

I chose the informal genre of an essay for my presentation in order to avoid a style overburdened with references, comparisons, and critiques, especially since this paper can only provide a sketchy outline of my theoretical framework.

The psychology of subjects in social practice

Psychic processes take place in individual subjects or persons. Hence a key task for psychology is to study persons. When psychologists study more encompassing societal practices, they must include the subjective personal aspects of those practices, so that what they study may remain part of psychology. This throws critical light on dominant research traditions: On the one hand groups, institutions, and other complex social practices are mostly studied without adequate conceptions of their subjective aspects; on the other hand the abstract, functionalist general psychology brackets the place of psychic processes in personal social practice. One might say that the psychology of personality should combine the theoretical disciplines of general psychology and social analysis and, furthermore, build a bridge to the various areas of applied psychology.

But research on the psychology of personality is fraught with recurring crises. They arise because theories are based on a conceptional gap between internal and external determinants. Internal individual properties (mostly personality traits and needs) are placed on one side, and external situational factors (conditions, stimuli, constraints) in the environment on the other. The only escape, it seems to many, would be to combine the two sides of the gap in ungainly mixtures of, say, internal properties exposed to external influences, etc. In psychology and related disciplines such methodologies and ensuing reductionisms are known under various names: Individualism and subjectivism versus social determinism and objectivism, to name but a few.

They all suffer from a common difficulty and deficit: How are we to grasp the ways in which persons develop their "properties", what they do in relation to their "external determinants", how they influence them, change them, and thus change their lives? When addressing such issues, they either fall back into objectivism and determinism, into endogenous subjectivism, or into pseudo-solutions which mix abstractions from the two sides, claiming that these factors "interact".

The concept of action in psychology

Following A. N. Leont'ev (1978), we may say that proponents of these views, strictly speaking, do not study living creatures. Evidently, at least to a Marxist, they must be studied in practice, activity – or action, as I prefer, following the work of "critical psychology" (Holzkamp, 1983). The concept of *action*, then, must be our key concept in the study of persons. Action is the third term, the missing link through which the two sides always are combined in practice. Within psychology several attempts have been made to give action a crucial role. To take action as our key concept, one might hope, should imply that psychology moves from considering form or structure as primary to the primacy of practical, relational contents. Nevertheless, two one-sided and mutually opposed, abstract approaches to the study of human action dominate which are unable to accomplish the change we need:

1. Almost all approaches within psychology consider the actions of a single individual in an immediate environment. Most do not even characterize the environment more precisely, but focus one-sidedly on the individual in the individual-environment relationship. They regard an isolated individual's detached actions, goals, intentions, plans, motives, thoughts, emotions, etc. and propose "laws" about this. Yet, such laws are about an abstraction – a ghost. Nobody lives and functions like that. Individuals are part of encompassing societal structures of re-production.

2. The opposite approach does include social structure, but in the guise of some conception of the actions of *the* individual in relation to *the* society. This is just another abstraction. It assumes a uniform relationship between two uniform entities which purportedly exists everywhere, and thus nowhere in particular. Since the impact of *the* society on *the* individual must be impressive, not to say overwhelming, according to such a view, it emphasizes constraining social determinants and construes *the* individual from outside and above. Nonetheless, individuals do not act from outside and above, uniformly in relation to *the* social structure. They are located in particular, concrete places, and they act and experience the world differently from those locations.

Towards a psychology of the subject

We must conceive of individual subjects in social practice from the standpoint and perspective of local agents. "Critical psychology" espouses such a general science of the subject from a first person standpoint. This approach has developed in parallel with other more or less similar positions in psychology and neighbouring disciplines. My research contributes to its expansion, in part by drawing upon such related work.

Some believe that to include a *subjective perspective* necessarily leads to methodological individualism. This is not the case. The "science of the subject", as developed in critical psychology, allows us to break out of that unfortunate trap by combining the subjective perspective of individuals with conceptions about the encompassing social practice in which subjects participate. However, the idea is not to avoid one trap only to fall into another. We must also insist that there is no such thing as a supra-individual psychological process. To study psychological processes, psychology must locate them at the level of individuals. The particular subject matter of the discipline of psychology unfolds at this level. Further, we must be careful not to confuse analytic distinctions, concerning "the human psyche", with the real connections in which these analytically distinguished aspects invariably exist. We must not turn analytic units, which cannot exist on their own, into "real things". We shouldn't imbue them with an existence of their own in concrete practice or consider them to be underlying "essences" which determine concrete practice. Psychological phenomena must be interpreted and integrated within an encompassing interdisciplinary approach to research on human social practice. Indeed, we can only really combine the study of psychic processes and social practice from a first person standpoint and perspective in social practice since that is how they are combined in practice by subjects. In short, we must conceptualize psychic processes as aspects of the actions of located subjects in ongoing social practice.

This point of view on individual psychological processes takes us beyond the prevailing, anonymous general psychology of psychological functions into a personal psychology, one that articulates each subject's first person perspective on the social context in which the subject is located and on that subject's actions, thoughts, emotions, etc. in it. Indeed, the world is given to every subject in "my first person perspective". So theoretical research must adopt a generalized first person standpoint in order to develop concepts suitable for each of us to use to make sense of our local practice from our perspective. This is not only so for the various areas of "individual psychology", but also for, say, social psychology. Here too the issue is whether we adopt the third person standpoint of a social psychology "from outside and above" or a first person social psychology in the plural. We should not lose sight of the constellations of first person psychological processes in interrelated, interacting, co-thinking and -feeling subjects. Nor should we regard these processes as free-floating, that is as bracketing the significance of their concrete locations in social practice. These conclusions also hold for the social psychology of groups, institutions, etc.

Evidently, theoretical conceptions about *the* individual (in some cases supplemented by *the* activity) in relation to *the* society are dislocated, decontextualized, deinstitutionalized abstractions. They are imbedded in a container metaphor of society which regards society primarily as a structure and, above that, as a totality beyond concrete space and time.

Subjects on location

To adopt the standpoint and perspective of the subject the way we propose, requires, instead, to introduce a concept of *location*. We cannot combine the study of subjects with the study of social practice in any robust way if we conceive of subjective perspectives as free-floating images. Invariably they are subjective perspectives from concrete locations in social practice. They are anchored in social space and time. My perspective is always from a location where I presently find myself. It is embodied from the place where I am now. In talk, thought, and imagination I may, of course, transpose my perspective into other times and places, but that presupposes its present location in the first place. To approach the study of human subjectivity and social practice through the concept of action, then, requires more than that we study them as phenomena in time, as, for instance, in narrative theories. Time does not exist by itself, but as spaces of time in time-space. And so does action. It takes place in social space and time as we move around and from one location to another.

To particular locations belong particular structures of relevance. The latter are particular, locally structured parts of encompassing social structures. The meaning of being at particular locations, then, differs, including the meaning of what can be done with particular local possibilities and which goals and interests are at stake in them. Local subjective perspectives relate to these particular local *structures of meaning*. They are subjective perspectives on structures of relevance for the located subject.

Subjects in contexts of action

Locations are incorporated in particular contexts of action. A *context of action* stands in particular relations to more encompassing societal structures of social practice. It is a common set of conditions and the locus for its participants' actions which re-produce and change it.

The concept of context of action is a preliminary common denominator for a set of more differentiated concepts about ongoing social practice. I prefer it to concepts such as situation, setting, field, or sector because it explicitly points to the basic role of action in my theoretical perspective. Social structures, social conditions, indeed, societies do not exist independently of, but, precisely, by virtue of their participants' actions to re-produce and change them. In coming to understand social practice, I contend, actions must lie at the basis of what we address and confront. Until recently, social theory neglected to unfold a more differentiated conception of societal practice, of the infrastructures of ongoing practice in concrete social times and places.

Clearly, contexts of action may exist more or less in passing; they may be, or become, institutionalized in a variety of ways. In any case, they are brought into practice by a greater or lesser number of participants. Their *goals* and *stakes* are realized in *plural*, by inter-acting participants.

For its participants an action context is characterized by a particular, more or less limited *scope* of *action possibilities*. Basically we regard social conditions not as external determinants or constraints, but as the, more or less restricted, objective scope of action possibilities. This holds for the re-production of action contexts as well as their change. Furthermore, the notion of "scope" directs our attention to issues concerning which possibilities are at hand for changing and developing participants' scopes, depending upon participants' degree of *disposal* over their context of action.

As stated earlier, every person participates in a context of action from his or her location. In practice these locations may constitute a set of prestructured, interrelated *positions*. Positions are a sub-category or specification of locations in the sense that we proceed from a quasi-physical definition of space and time to the level of a societally organized and institutionalized space and time and its implications for subjects' practice. A set of possible, more or less clearly interrelated positions may belong to an existing social context of action. To varying degrees, participants may select among them, neglect, and change them. From their particular locations and positions, participants have particular scopes of personal action possibilities, optional *contributions*, *interests*, and perspectives in relation to the present context. This applies to the re-production and change of the context as well as to their lives, and the lives of some or all other participants, in relation to it. So participant interests and optional contributions depend upon their particular part in disposing over the context.

Subjects as participants

To unfold concepts which basically regard the subject or person as a *participant*, implies to study closely a person's particular way to participate in, to be a particular part of, to partake of a context in a *particular* and only *partial* way in relation to the practice of that context, the realization of its goals, its re-production and change, etc. It propels us to consider both personal modes of functioning and the meaning of personal participation to be partial and particular in relation to a context.

After all, the *goals* of a context of action are not realized solely by one participant, but by a plurality of participants in a particular, located, and positioned interrelationship. What happens in the context, even the *consequences* of my own actions, do not depend directly and exclusively upon my individual actions and *intentions*. It is not only up to me. This claim implies a fundamental critique of any abstract-individual conception of individual action, goals, plans, intentions, etc. A person is no "autonomous unit" in the sense that its functioning and structure can be conceived of by itself. Every person is a participant. As a participant, a person must direct his or her actions and intentions according to the scope of his or her particular, anticipated part in the practice of the context and the consequences he or she may aim to realize or, conversely, fear to come true.

As a subject, I specify and articulate my particular goals, interests, etc. in relation to the overall goals, etc. of the context. From my particular position, I have particular possibilities, interests, and *reasons* to participate in it. Out of this particularity I configure my particular stakes in the context. Individual possibilities, interests, perspectives, knowledge, and stances become particular ones. Individual action and awareness are not omnipotent and all-encompassing. They are particular and partial phenomena. So if we want to assess the consciousness, meaning, knowledge, reasons, and abilities which subjects actually bring to bear, we need to approach them from their local position in relation to the context. We cannot merely attribute knowledge and reasons to them from some position outside or above them – say, some researcher's position. That would not tell us in which partial ways particular participants configure their particular perspectives and actions from their local positions in relation to the context.

Subjects in constellations of action

In order, among other things, to grasp how subjects configure their relationship to the contexts in which they take part, we must distinguish analytically between a context of action and a *constellation of action*. Every participating subject considers and evaluates his or her relationship to the context, to other participants in it, and to the events which may come to pass or which they may bring about, by relating their own actions to the actions of others during their course of action. We each weigh, evaluate, and direct our actions with and against each other in some emerging constellation of actions. In addition, a constellation of actions is but one among several possible concrete realizations of the given scope of the context. Any context is realized and changed in particular and partial ways in the constellation which emerges out of the particular relationship between participants' actions. Indeed, constellations of action may be composed of actions which are more or less well-integrated, conjoined, coordinated, heterogeneous, even mutually opposed, conflicting, and contradicting.

Subjective action potency

The set of personal preconditions to participation in my position in the context of action is my *personal action potency*. While an action context defines the scope of objectively possible action for participants, the action potency defines the scope of subjectively possible action. But this is a relational definition. Indeed, only when taken together do we arrive at the practical *scope of action*. Subjective potencies are only so in relation to what is objectively possible in an action context. The subjective action potency is defined locally in relation to what it requires of me to be able to participate in the action context from my position and in relation to what other participants are able to do in our constellation of actions. It is defined concretely, relationally, contextually, and positionally. What psychology ordinarily designates as "properties" of the person, are aspects of the action potency. They develop as aspects of it and may contribute to its further development. Potentiality and modifiability are crucial features of properties, capacities, and abilities. As a subject, I may develop my action potency in order to extend my participation in the context and in our disposal over it, in order to follow changing demands and possibilities in it, and to take part in developing it and my scope of participation. Just as objective possibilities are characterized by a particular dual pattern through which participants both act within and dispose over and extend them, so my subjective action potency is characterized by a particular pattern of ways to act within and take part in extending present objective scopes.

To make action potency the core concept in characterizing subjective preconditions, emphasizes the practical nature of subjectivity. The conditions of possibility for human consciousness are rooted in personal participation in social practice. Basically a person is not defined by some stipulated ability for reflection, self-consciousness, identity, a self, second order desires, or whatever, but by those properties necessary to be able to participate in complex societal practice. Reflexive consciousness, then, is conceived as the necessary first person perspective and standpoint on my context of action (in its encompassing connections), my position and participation in it, our constellation of actions, and the meaning of all this for each of us, including me.

We may pursue this approach into the study of the particular *psychic functional aspects* of personal action potency. Personal *thinking* consists of directed, hopefully mutually related and coordinated, thought processes from participants' particular positions in the constellation of actions in the context. My analytic aims of thinking and the significance of my thoughts depend upon what other participants do and think, and upon the kind of context we are in. My thinking depends upon the kind of analytic aims we set ourselves in that context, and upon the way we distribute and coordinate them. Our thinking and knowledge, then, are not merely individual, nor merely distributed among us. They are interrelated, negotiated, disputed, and contested in a particular constellation. Likewise, our personal thinking and knowledge are partial and located. Furthermore, the relationship between my personal *observation* and thinking is mediated by what is immediately at hand, but also by things not directly available from my particular position and perspective in my particular context. In my thinking I include those aspects of social practice which are not immediately observable and available to me in my present time and space, and I relate them to my ongoing observations and actions.

The same holds for *emotions*. My present, complex emotional state is a particular, concretely located, subjective evaluation of how I am where I am now. It emanates from my present location in relation to others in a particular context and expresses my evaluation of its particular relevance structure to me. In a more or less encompassing way, then, my emotional state reflects my overall evaluation of the context, my possible meaning for it, and its possible meaning for me from my present location in it. In so doing, my emotions reach selectively and re-constructively into my past and stretch anticipatingly into the future as my motivation or coercion to act in particular ways. As in the case of thinking, when I transpose my frame of evaluation in time and space, my emotional processes do, of course, rest on and incorporate my present location.

Cross-contextual structures of social practice

At this point we must extend our analytic framework for subjects' social practice one step further. We talked about *the* action context as if there were but one. Or, to put it differently, as if the context were an isolated island. That, of course, is yet another abstraction. In reality, action contexts are part of more encompassing *structures of social practice*. This is the case in any complex societal structure of ongoing practice. In fact, only when we cease to consider action contexts one at a time, do we move beyond "container" notions of contexts.

At issue here are particular notions of social structure. More and less institutionalized and transitory contexts of action are objectively related in particular ways, thus making up particular social structures. Particular *connections* and *disconnections* exist among them and allow us to elaborate notions of societal *infrastructures* of ongoing social practice. We need to work out which connections and disconnections exist between which contexts among a multitude of social contexts. To do so, we must focus not only on existing connections and *intersections*, but on particular *separations* and *barriers* among them. And we must work out their *diversity, heterogeneity*, and *contradictions*.

This argument rests on the contention that social structures do not exist independently of social practice. They are structures of social practice which are re-produced and changed through human social action. We need a concept of structure that does not depict it as external to practice, but as the structure of social practice. Structural conditions, constraints, and demands are not external to practice, but rather aspects of ongoing practice. A theory of society can only distinguish structure and action analytically.

In complex structures of societal practice, particular contexts of action may be organized to take care of particular *goals* and *affairs* and assigned paricular *tasks* for a particular society, particular members and participants. Members differentiate and structure their societal practice across space and time in relation to such arrangements.

All this has multiple implications for subjects' actions, not only for the present participants in a particular context of action, but for potential and more or less passing participants as well. To what degree, from where, for whom, and for which purposes contexts are open or closed, defines – more or less modifiable – particular scopes of action and modes of *access* and *sequestration, inclusion* and *exclusion*. These define which personal action possibilities are available and which personal action potencies are necessary for pursuing particular interests, stakes, and goals in and across particular contexts.

To put it differently, *power* over contexts and inter-contextual relations as well as *influence* upon them are exercised by organizing these contexts and inter-contextual relations in particular ways. Power restricts influence over contexts to particular parties and particular ends while closing them off, keeping them separate, keeping other potential participants out, constraining their access and the ends they are able to pursue. In this way, participation in contexts and the optional use thereof in the pursuit of one's interests are controlled and unevenly distributed; also contradictory interests are accentuated among involved parties. On the other hand, influence over contexts may be *democratized* by extending connections among them, common access to them, scopes in them, and disposal over them in the pursuit of common goods. Along these lines, we may pursue a democratic perspective on social practices and their development.

Multiple participation across contexts

The extension of our analytic framework to encompass a plurality of contexts calls for a similar extension of the study of subjects in social practice. Literally speaking, it is misleading to conceive of subjects as merely being in a location, or position, even in a particular context of action. So they are, some of the time, while standing, sitting, lying around, etc. But, clearly, acting subjects often move around in and across contexts. They participate in more than one. There is a striking silence about this in psychology. Personal practice is not studied as concrete movement in social space and time. Concepts of the person are of creatures seemingly immobile in social space. According to some conceptions, persons do move in time, through the span of their life-histories. But these conceptions conceive of time without social space, an abstraction of time, an abstract trajectory in time. Still, it is a basic practical condition of being a human subject to participate in complex and encompassing re-productive structures of social practice. In relation to these objective structures of practice, persons structure their possibilities, actions, and the subjective meaning of participation in diverse contexts. Of course, this does not eliminate the local and positioned character of personal practice. It merely sets it on the move.

As mentioned earlier, various contexts of action typically play different parts in attending to particular societal goals and affairs. They are diverse and heterogeneous. Facing them, subjects confront different stakes, interests, and scopes of participation. Their access to action contexts and their influence upon them differ as do their positions and potencies for participating in them. So contexts have different meanings to subjects, and their goals and subjective reasons to participate in them differ. To put it briefly, (aside from variations in the ways different subjects participate in the same context which we dealt with above) the same subject participates in different ways in diverse contexts. As a subject moves across contexts, he or she varies his or her mode of participation, according to the particular nature of the present context, the subject's position in it, and the stakes he or she pursues. Indeed, a subject often has good reasons to participate in different ways in different contexts. All of this, creates a high degree of complexity and heterogeneity in the practice of every subject.

Mediations of subjects' local practice

Any subject moves more or less routinely and deliberately from one context to another. Subjects pursue their configurations of goals and interests across contexts. Sometimes they pursue a particular goal and interest across contexts. These moves are incorporated in more or less recurrent patterns of the everyday time-space of our personal practice, to which persons add moves into particular, less frequent, occasional, or one-time-only places. Indeed, we often participate in a particular context mainly for reasons that are aimed at realizing goals and interests which primarily originate in and "belong" to another context. In so doing, we make use of particular connections that exist between these contexts, or that we and others create and extend, and that make it possible to pursue goals and interests in one context by taking part in another in a particular way. In fact, this is another neglected feature in theories of subjects' social practice. Human action has a potential and varying cross-contextual scope, scale, or reach.

On the one hand, then, participant actions, goals, and intentions are localized phenomena. I always am in a local position with its perspective on current relations and events, including my part in them. My actions, goals, and intentions unfold in particular ways in particular contexts, often for good reasons. On the other hand, we do not bring about these subjective variations by operating, so to speak, a switchboard of contextual roles. There are particular subjective connections at play in our pursuit of a subjective configuration of goals and interests or a particular goal and interest across time and space. The subjective meaning of participating in a particular way and the subjective reasons for doing so, do not exclusively originate in and "belong" to the present location. They include concerns of a cross-contextual nature, stretching into social space and time. Hence a subject's current action in the present context is partial in yet another sense beyond those discussed earlier: It is part of his or her more encompassing participation in interrelated societal contexts. It is incorporated in his or her short- and long-term trajectories across contexts.

Due to the cross-contextual nature of individual existence, subjects are bound to take *direct* as well as *indirect* relationships into account in their local action. In order to configure their local reasons for action and to direct their local action in their present context, subjects compose local constellations of direct and indirect concerns. Thus subjects' direct, immediate relationships and actions are *mediated* by indirect ones in localized ways. Subjects include indirect relationships in particular ways in order to achieve particular ends in their present context. For the same reasons they may tell about and account for aspects of their lives in other times and places in particular ways. Moreover, in the present context they may pursue ends which reach beyond its boundaries aiming at particular effects they wish to achieve or seek to avoid in other times and places. Indeed, the inclusion of indirect relationships is essential to the way subjects, with more or less deliberate intentions, bring about indirect effects in some other time and place. Subjects allow indirect relationships to influence their immediate action in a way they hold necessary and suitable to bring about the spreading indirect effects they seek to propel. This cross-contextual mediation of individual action is another familiar feature of everyday personal practice and of the functioning of many social institutions. It is often neglected in studies of the practice of subjects and institutions. Subjects' present action is influenced by and also may influence relationships in other times and places. In allowing for this, subjects link the goals, stakes, and interests they pursue as participants in different contexts of action. Indeed, the other contexts from which they include concerns or into which they seek to bring about effects may be ones in which they themselves participate or in which only other participants in the present context take part.

We may pursue this line of analysis into the study of psychic functions. Individual subjects configure and define their thought processes inter-contextually. They negotiate, coordinate, and contest them inter-subjectively. And their thoughts unfold in an ongoing constellation of actions in a local context. Likewise, a participant's emotional state is a complex evaluation, composed of mediations between his or her present location and his or her indirect relations in time and space. Indeed, the potentialities of complex human thinking and emotionality unfold along the dimensions of locally evaluated, anticipated, and remembered trajectories in social time and space.

Socially mediated subjective complexity

Evidently, the complex social mediation of individual phenomena does not undo and replace a first person standpoint. It remains a necessary grounding and perspective for individual subjects' located participation in social practice. But the meaning of a present context to its participants varies, in part because the other contexts in which they participate, or the ways they participate in them, differ. There is a distinct unfolding structure to particular subjects' overall participation in social practice which gives the present context a specific status and meaning in their practice. Each subject must identify its relative significance for his or her particular purposes, or for the mode of life he or she takes part in sustaining and developing through his or her practice in and across contexts. In some contexts, then, some subjects participate in ways which must primarily be understood from their other contexts. There is a structure of relevance at play here, based upon the meaning of a subject's particular participation for the way he or she sustains, unfolds, and develops his or her social practice. And this individual structure of relevance is part of the particular, local, and cross-contextual (but socio-structurally mediated) form of life in which that individual is a particular participant.

To the person, the complex, cross-contextual, diverse, even contested nature of his or her participation accentuates the issue of which interconnections among his or her activities are relevant in order to sustain, unfold, and develop his or her practice: How do I avoid acting at cross-purposes with some of my own goals, acting disconnectedly, acting in total self-contradiction, or stumbling over my own feet in pursuit of my interests and goals? In a particular context, how do I keep my stakes together, connect my actions, interests, and goals, separate what I believe needs separating, structure my affairs as I see fit, also in relation to others' activities and stances across space and time? This amounts to a personal endeavour to a) sustain a sufficient measure of interconnection among my complex activities, b) in so doing, to consider the objective interrelations of contextual activities, and c) to secure a sufficient measure of overall integration of individual sustenance and development in my changing scopes, activities, and potencies. In doing all this, I relate subjective and objective aspects of my practice.

However, it would be mistaken to believe that these issues of subjective complexity, integration, and development turn an individual subject into a "multiple personality", a chameleon, or a fully integrated unity with no loose ends, ruptures, or contradictions. Probably every individual subject expands and accentuates common features in its preferred modes of approaching and participating in even partly diverse contexts – thus providing an extra measure of individual, subjective parsimony, so to speak. And it is a basic practical necessity to sustain a sufficient measure of subjective interconnection. Any subject must struggle to keep a grip on his or her trajectory in the particular ways in which he or she moves around in, and across, societal contexts of action. Yet, personalism and related holisms in psychological theories of personality oversimplify matters by presuming that an "integrated" person is an internal, strictly personal "unity" in which everything is synthesized in perfect wholeness – a sort of person it is easier to imagine in others, especially in those we do not know well. Actually, any subject is more complex than that – differentiated, varied, incomplete, full of ruptures, conflicts, and contradictions. This is what any subject must try to hold on to, in ways that are suitable for sustaining and extending his or her grip on his or her complex and diverse existence. In personalism, personal cohesion is not primarily considered a practical matter, but turned into a merely internal, mental, or even spiritual matter. To presume that purely conceptual or spiritual integration may be obtained, is to simplify the diversity of subjects' social practice and, in effect, to abstract and detach the issue of personal integration from the objective relations of concrete practice. If we conceive it to be a purely cognitive achievement, we turn cognitive categories into free-floating generalities.

Subjective standpoints

From their practice in local contexts, subjects evaluate, articulate, connect, and generalize the premises of their participation and points of view on social practice in its local, contextual diversity. Thus, a subject actively adopts, elaborates, and composes a personal *standpoint* or stance. It is a stand I take in, to, and across the mediated social contexts of my trajectory, and it allows me to direct my actions as coherently as possible, to connect and configure my diverse participations in diverse contexts and at different times. My standpoint is not merely a passive result of my, more or less typical, objective conditions and positions. I may develop and modify it. And I may work it out and over more or less deliberately and coherently, drawing upon the always more encompassing practical background for my articulated standpoints. Sometimes I adopt a particular standpoint merely "in passing", though. Its reach into other times and places, participants and parties may, indeed, differ. It is never final and complete.

Though I elaborate my standpoint from local foundations in the first place, it stretches across time and place from where I am now. Still, it gives me good reasons to act, think, and feel differently in different times and places, depending upon the particular context, my participation, and upon the place they occupy in the interrelated contexts of my trajectory in social practice. It is no contradiction in terms to say both that a standpoint stretches across time and space to articulate and pursue connections among them, and that it also gives me good reasons to act, think, and feel differently across time and space. On the contrary, that is part of living a complex life. A standpoint, then, is no fixed structure of traits or goals, but a configuration of more general premises through which I direct my social practice. I combine it, more or less flexibly, with my particular current context, needs and interests to guide the subjective structuration and direction of my particular activities.

In fact, a subject adopts a complex structure of more or less coherently and deliberately interconnected standpoints. I weigh and interrelate my standpoints in accordance with the structures of relevancies of my complex practice in order to sustain and develop my participation in a local, mediated form of life. I work out, articulate, coordinate, negotiate, and contest my structure of standpoints with other participants and other parties in societal practice. The fundamental condition of possibility which allows this process to take place, is what we have called a "generalized first person standpoint". The subjective stances I take may be more or less opposed, particular or general, depending upon whether their premises are opposed to the premises of others, encompass particular parties, or may, indeed, be shared by everyone. In order to be able to take part in changing present positions, contexts, and structures, we must take stances, more or less in accord with those others take. We negotiate, fight, engage in conflict and oppose, make alliances and join together over them.

So my complex standpoints are no purely cognitive features, but features of my ongoing actions. They do remain attached to and are elaborated, articulated, and pursued in my local participation in and across time and space. Still, I do not work out my personal standpoints independently of existing societal forms of thinking, linguistic and cultural forms, social knowledge, other existing stances, etc. Neither must I, nor do I, just take them over or subsume myself to them. Rather, I take my stances in relation to societal forms and include them in so doing. Compared to them, my personal standpoints remain restricted and partial, with areas left more or less unaddressed or indistinct.

Socially mediated subjective conflicts

Contradictions and *conflicts* abound in societal practice, across and within contexts, among its various parties, and about and for its subjects. The present context may be contested and made an object of struggle. Various constellations of common and opposed interests may be at stake. All of this affects the goals of the context, participants' reasons for taking part in them in particular ways, and the standpoints they adopt in relating to them. In order to identify a perspective that may allow us to overcome these conflicts, we must adopt, elaborate, and pursue a generalized standpoint.

Although conflicts play an important role in everyday practice, they play a strikingly minor one in personality theories which mostly consider "personality" and "personality development" merely to be a kind of "task". Instead, we must conceptualize personality development as conflictual. Its direction and course is not straigthforward, but a contested, zig-zagging one, marked by progressions and retrogressions. It takes place in social contexts, marked by opposed interests among participants. These conflicts turn subjective reasons for action into conflicting ones and create numerous forms of personal ambiguities and alternating standpoints and voices, which can only be disentangled and located with great difficulty. They make it difficult for us to predetermine the consequences of intended actions and create intersubjective and subjective discords and contests of interpretation about events, reasons, and personality properties. They personalize discords and instrumentalize intersubjective relations, filling them with compromises, compensations, unequal benefits, and sacrifices. They also affect our socio-cultural notions of love, care, and service.

Conflicts may set their stamp on interpretations of the present context of action, of particular participants' significance for its state of affairs, and of their reasons for participating in particular ways. Indeed, interpretations may become a method by which participants engage in conflicts and in struggles for power over the context. By being subjected to conflicts of interpretation, the significance of the context for particular participants, their own evaluations and standpoints with respect to their actions, intentions, reasons, goals, properties, thoughts, emotions, etc. become complicated and entangled. Especially in conflict, multiparty practices are often interpreted – even theorized – from particular positions which are not made explicit and amenable to common reflection. Particular parties more or less monopolize interpretation and may instrumentalize it as a particular way to pursue particular interests. Then confounded perspectives of interpretation, action, and account spread among participants.

Socially mediated subjective trajectories

As my line of argument has unfolded, we have gradually related physical time-space and societally organized time-space to subjective *trajectories*. These trajectories are not trajectories in pure time, though, abstracted from the social structures of space. The meanings of and reasons for concrete participation depend on more than their locus in such an abstract "story". Rather my trajectory takes place in and across concrete social locations, positions, and contexts. In its course I move in and across places, and my trajectory of locations is part of ongoing socio-historical practice. Some societally prestructured dimensions of inter-contextual relations furnish an objective structure to my trajectory, in relation to which I structure and unfold it in practice. Thus, trajectories relate objective and subjective aspects, on an individual-historical scale, of existing and changing structures of social practice. Besides, my trajectory of participation has meanings that go beyond the personal. It has meanings in and for social practice since in the course of my daily life I pursue particular goals, interests, and standpoints in particular contexts of social practice. My partial participation has meaning to me, to others, in and for particular contexts, to our society, and to the common good. There is a societal dimension to the standpoints and meanings of the trajectory I pursue. In other words, there is a social dimension to my identity, reasons, knowledge, potentialities, cognitive and emotional processes. In defining it, I relate my present possibilities and potencies to those of others, and to other contexts in the structure of societal practice. In this more or less global perspective, I identify opposed, partial, and common features of our interests and standpoints. In short, my trajectory is firmly anchored in the history of local social practice and its mediations, where it, too, may become a matter of mutual, personal conflicts.

Analysis of psycho-social practice

Having outlined some main features of my analytic framework, let me now briefly indicate what kind of questions it enables us to address and to what kinds of research it may lead. As I said in the beginning, it is designed for use where it is essential to combine psychological and social science studies of human practice. In my book, I used it to re-search the psycho-social practice of psychotherapy from various major positions and perspectives in turn. Here I will try to sketch, very briefly, some common features and main points of the analytic approach developed in much greater detail in the book. My analyses are founded on my empirical studies of ongoing therapeutic practice, studies of the training and clinical supervision of therapists, and on materials from a series of research conferences convened to study psychological practice.

Therapeutic modes of operation

Predominant forms of thinking and research about therapeutic practice construe and account for therapy outcomes as effects of the therapist's doings in the encounter. The therapist is some sort of a *maker* of therapeutic proceedings and outcomes. Notions of therapeutic *expertise* and the therapeutic *mode of operation* are marked by abstract individualism. If we take their word for it, therapy is a *profession-centered* service in which professionals, when it comes down to it, more or less *monopolize* interventions and interpretations and, thus, misconstrue and lose sight of many of their clients' activities and interpretations. Within the action contexts of therapy sessions, the participants' actual, multiple first person perspectives and standpoints are entangled and confounded – in a practice nevertheless claimed to be executed for the good of the client.

The analytic framework I developed offers quite a different approach to the study of therapeutic practice. Like many other institutionalized societal practices, it is the goal of therapy to improve problematic aspects of clients' lives in their everyday contexts outside the therapy encounters. So in my research on this multi-contextual practice, I investigated not only the complex inter-action in clients' and therapists' immediate *encounters* in therapy sessions, but also clients' *everyday lives* and therapists' *institutional working contexts*. If there were no connections among these contexts, encounters could have no effects on clients' everyday practices. Given my theoretical framework, it is obviously essential to examine the interrelationships between these contexts and parties in order to develop a new and more comprehensive approach to the mode of operation of therapy, and, more generally, of institutions in relation to their *users*.

Decentered analysis of practice

To clients, the context of the therapy encounter which they share with their therapists, is a peculiar, additional, temporary "time-off" sort of context. If we consider the constellation of contexts in and across which clients participate, other contexts are more significant for their personal social existence, including which problems they run into and their possibilities to address and overcome them. In other words, the therapeutic encounter lies outside clients' primary contexts where therapeutic impacts, nevertheless, first of all are to be realized. So it is the main objective for therapy encounters to be of significance for clients' actions, reasons, relations, trajectories, etc. in contexts which are customarily viewed by therapists as outside and elsewhere. The mode of operation of therapy action contexts on clients' everyday lives is mostly indirect and mediated. In fact, we must *decenter* our comprehension of the effects of therapy and focus on how clients may locate and anchor its cross-contextual impacts in their main everyday contexts. To understand the operation of therapy, we must, first of all, approach it from clients' positions in their primary everyday contexts. Ordinarily, conditions, events, and processes outside the immediate therapy encounter are crucial in determining whether and for what *clients use it*, i.e. its concrete effects. The main processes take place outside, in between, and afterwards. In spite of this, mostly the therapeutic mode of operation is regarded as a matter of *transfer* from the encounter which is, thus, misleadingly presumed to be clients' primary context. Also transfer is generally presumed to occur, but rarely researched in a comprehensive way. Instead, we need a broader, decentered approach which rests on a comprehensive view of clients as acting and experiencing subjects in and across their social contexts. Treatment is a problematic part of conflicting everyday contexts. In fact, it obtains its actual meanings precisely by being so. This should lead us to consider how it is included or excluded in everyday contexts, and how its meanings are contested here. The contested, indirect workings of therapy follow changes outside of it and in relation to it as, mostly, only a secondary part thereof.

In the secondary context of the therapy encounter clients include phenomena and concerns from other places. Their state of well-being, perspectives, interests, reasons, and actions in therapy sessions are mediated. More or less deliberately and conflictingly, clients may direct their actions within therapy encounters, in an attempt to achieve more or less clearly anticipated, indirect effects on their lives in their main everyday contexts, at other times and places. In so doing, they take into account particular features of the immediate context of the encounter. They are concerned with which objective connections and disconnections exist between the encounter and their other contexts, which connections they may influence and create, and which they may prevent. Though they deal with their conflicts in several contexts, they do so differently, depending upon the concrete meanings of the context at hand and its connections with their other contexts. Their state of well-being, interests, standpoints, and actions vary across contexts because of these differences and interconnections. Their conflicts have different meanings to them in different contexts. In order to pursue their interests clearly, it is important to them to determine which particular restrictions and possibilities encounters offer. In all this, the standpoint from which they participate in the encounter is mediated. The question is: How do clients include aspects and effects of their primary contexts in the therapy encounters in the ways that they give accounts of participation in those contexts, and in the ways they functionalize encounters? And how do clients use encounters to introduce changes into their conflicting everyday contexts?

Therapeutic analysis

If we consider the constellation of contexts in and across which therapists participate in social practice, there is a different structure of relevance at play than that of their clients'. Of course, therapists and clients alike are citizens of a society, and as such they are related to, connected with and separated from each other in common and diverse circumstances. As citizens, other contexts than their professional working contexts form part of therapists' social practice. But the prevailing practice and ideology of professionalism brackets the significance of therapists' lives as citizens. It transforms their therapeutic practice to make it stand out as separated from, and from that position directed at clients' everyday lives while being involved in societal, institutional power structures in a less tangible and accessible way. As professionals, then, therapists carry out their therapeutic practice as seen from their working contexts, and their professional, institutional contexts are their primary contexts. Their professional perspectives, interests, reasons, tasks, standpoints, etc. in the encounter are mediated through these other contexts. Hence, interactions between therapists and clients in encounters are marked by diverse mediations from each their opposite primary contexts. Their perspectives and standpoints are mediated from opposite primary directions. The intersubjective exchange of perspectives between them is a significant part of the processes by which encounters obtain effects, but these perspectives are mediated in *opposite* ways. In order to understand their intersubjectivity in the therapy encounter, we must recognize these opposite mediations. Since therapists' interests, perspectives, and standpoints in the encounter are primarily mediated through their working context, while therapy is primarily to be directed at clients' everyday contexts, a *diversion* of therapists' concerns may arise. This may create problems of perspectives, interests, and standpoints for therapists, especially when their working context and their clients' everyday contexts appear to stand in a relation of (partial) conflict. The former may then inhibit and disturb rather than enable client treatment. Uncontrolled and unadmitted switching between standpoints and perspectives may occur.

Since my aim is to develop analytic means which therapists may use to think through and develop their practice, let us briefly look at the analytic features of therapeutic competence, i.e. therapeutic modes of thinking. A more comprehensive standpoint on psycho-social practice must lead to correspondingly more comprehensive *modes of thinking*. As is the case for all human thinking, therapeutic thinking does not occur in abstract heads. It follows us around in our social practice. It is localized, positioned, and in perspective, and from here it is related to our ongoing observations. It interchanges with the thinking of others' present and with the materials and means of thinking at our disposal in the current context. Among other things by means of thinking, we establish connections between contexts and become able in one context to deal with and influence phenomena at other times and places. In our local doing and thinking, we draw particular connections between what we do and think in different contexts. Our thinking plays a crucial part in our recognition and deliberate use of objective connections in the world to pursue our tasks and interests and to influence them. In the case of a therapy encounter, it is primarily a matter of including problematic relations outside of it, in order to overcome them in those other contexts. We not only think in constellations within the encounter, but beyond them, into other contexts and back again. When we think about such comprehensive cross-contextual matters, we may realize their essential, internal connections. We accentuate particular connections and combine them into more comprehensive assumptions about the internal connections, relevant for defining problems and opening up new possibilities of action. We make them less equivocal and generalize them.

In the processes of thinking within therapeutic encounters, therapists should recognize and make use of the fact that not only they do the thinking. Therapeutic thinking is distributed and coordinated. It is an intersubjective process, negotiated among its participants who are in different positions, with different interests and perspectives on current conflicts and possibilities. Disputes may occur over what to accentuate and generalize, i.e. over which assumptions are important and general to understand, and which might influence current conflicts and possibilities. We re-examine, dispute, reject and question, modify, piece together, recognize, confirm, etc. each others' contributions. When we manage to create an interconnected construction, it remains heterogeneously constructed, maybe even intersubjectively disputed, differently conceived and used – although, when successful, we combine our views, at least enough that some form of coordinated or joint action among us becomes possible. In any case, if we want to overcome current conflicts, we need to relate and combine our thoughts about them.

We think about problems as parts of social practice in a more comprehensive sense and include other social contexts, interests, experiences, and standpoints in the way we think through problems and possibilities. We also include absent parties' actions, thoughts, etc. in our local thinking. Moreover, we relate our thoughts to encompassing societal forms of thinking. In our personal thinking we include and may contribute to societal knowledge, disputes, alliances, developments, etc. Still, our personal thinking remains partial. It is characterized by particular points of emphasis and areas unthought of. We should recognize these differences in positions, approaches, and partiality in relation to our current conflicts when we relate and combine our efforts to think them through. We each adopt partial standpoints, negotiate and combine them with others' partial standpoints.

The above arguments are more comprehensive than what therapists normally accomplish in practice. In fact, they are so for good reasons. They are meant to enable us to analyse our current practice in the direction of developing a more far-ranging practice. Nevertheless, I contend, they unavoidably are part of current practice and not some abstract norms imposed upon it. This is so because the analyses point at existing scopes of possibilities which are not fully realized in current practice, but which practitioners and others involved may set themselves the goal to pursue and extend in the interest of improving therapeutic practice. Indeed, already in order to be able to carry out their everyday practice the way they do now, therapists must take them into consideration in more or less explicit, systematic, restricted, and transformed ways. At the same time, and contrary to this, they must keep a good deal of their thoughts in therapeutic sessions to themselves, and they must pretend they are the ones who have done all the responsible thinking when they account to outside parties and authorities for what they do. In their social practice therapists are caught in a *double bookkeeping* system concerning their thoughts and actions. The necessities of accountability and sole professional responsibility lie behind their mystifying "profession-centredness". This restricts and counteracts the necessary decentering of their practice and its analysis which is, nevertheless, called for.

Positioned concepts of mental illness

Let us now sketch some issues of analysis related to the psycho-social dimensions of concepts of mental illness. Since these concepts are used by practitioners, we must – from a standpoint of a science of the subject – inquire into practitioners' use of them in their local professional practice in relation to their clients. We must determine the function and place of their concept of illness in their social practice. Conceptions of illness have a special and limited place in their practice since the whole rationale of a social practice cannot be compressed within one personalized concept. Evidently, the professional concept of mental illness is used by one party from his position about another party in it. It reflects therapists' judgments about their clients. To comprehend the concept, we must consider the therapist and the use of the concept by the therapist in relation to the client. As already stated in general terms: In social practice we face a plurality of interrelated subject standpoints. A party's concepts are part of his or her dealings with his or her practice from his or her position, affected by his or her needs, interests, reasons for action, tasks, responsibilities, accountabilities, etc. In contrast, existing professional and theoretical concepts of mental illness seemingly stem from nowhere. They are abstracted from practice, decontextualized. This state of affairs is even seen as a guarantee of scientific objectivity, and it implies that practitioners do not appear in them. Therefore, such concepts offer therapists insufficient grounds to guide their own actions in concrete practice. They, and we, need a theory about professional subjectivity in context, or else the activities of diagnosis and therapy cannot really be combined.

Conflicts play a crucial role in the psycho-social dimensions of mental illness in clients' everyday life. Psycho-social practice pursues the task of finding such conflicts and helping to realize possibilities to overcome them, primarily in clients' everyday contexts "out there". This is what a concept of subjects' mental illness should primarily address. My reasons to become ill are grounded in conflicts among participants in my social practice. If they were not, I, or we, would already have overcome the trouble. As it is, conflicts make us block each others' ways and get stuck in various constellations. We prevent the resolution of our interpersonal and personal conflicts, for reasons which have to do with the contrary possibilities and interests of our respective positions in our context. Perspectives become dislocated and entangled. Often some participants are put under pressure to reinterpret their views. Participants may gradually come to articulate reasons for their actions from the perspective of other dominating positions. My standpoint becomes a mixture and confusion of dislocated perspectives and interests, of voices seemingly without clear local grounding, thinking all sorts of things from different angles. This seems typical of clients' ways of being confused and getting lost. When a client's standpoint gets entangled in these conflicts, it becomes problematic and unreliable. He or she must seek to disentangle and reconstruct the plurality of perspectives involved in it.

Mental illness is not first of all a personal attribute or property. It is something I am in my context. It primarily has concrete, practical meanings for me and other participants. Put differently, everyday ways of being mentally ill are the practical basis for concepts about mental illness. Contrary to this, in the forms of thinking of prevalent professional concepts of mental illness, it is somebody else's judgment about me, my properties, subjective state, and behaviors. Such professional concepts bracket differences between my perspective and, in particular, the perspective of professional judgment. My mental illness is reinterpreted from their position. Hence, my own perpective on it may become further mixed up, confounded and heterogeneous.

Since existing concepts implicitly are construed from particular locations, we must comprehend them reflexively as concepts articulated from there, and as being about complex multiparty practices across contexts. Furthermore, the various parties involved pursue partly diverse tasks because they participate primarily from positions in different social, institutional contexts. In psycho-social practice different parties meet and interrelate. They come from different primary contexts and different institutions. When they meet, they negotiate, cooperate, and fight over their diversely mediated concerns. When the parties move across social contexts, they "carry with them" the concerns and tasks of their primary institutions in mediated ways.

Positioned research practice

When the practice of particular research institutions and projects are connected with psycho-social practice, different relations may arise. These relations may be problematic and lead to conflict with and within the practice under study in ways which do not contribute much to its development. We need to unfold concepts and forms of research which are better suited to developing a more useful psycho-social practice. Much prior theorizing about the practice of therapy implicitly applies a researcher's or, at the most, some top professional agent's position, perspective, and standpoint to those clients and users for whose benefit this practice is claimed to be executed. When we use the concepts I have proposed to examine psycho-social practice, the theoretical problem becomes one of understanding all participants' diverse positions and diverse trajectories in relation to each other. These concepts direct us towards developing more democratic, user-oriented forms of research and practice. They propel us to ask how to organize practice in such a way that user access and influence may be increased and the direction of services towards users' everyday lives emphasized. This requires a commitment to shift our predominant ways of comprehending clients from a perspective that conceives them as patients to a perspective in which clients are viewed as users in social time-space, engaged in pursuing their concerns and goals.

In the book my framework forms the basis of a conception of *practice research*. Such research must investigate and analyse the interconnected personal perspectives on complex practices, of participants who find themselves in different, mutually related positions and contexts. It throws light on particular participants' different interests, possibilities, and reasons for participating in particular ways. These may then be made available to other participants. Participants may reconsider and reevaluate their reasons in light of the resulting relationship between their actions and the often surprisingly diverse significance which that which takes place has to each of them. Our research may focus on the concrete constellations of actions, problems, and possibilities which arise among and for the parties in a context, and point to possibilities by which participant actions could be combined to improve their grasp on common goals.

Such research is geared to produce results which participants may use to identify, handle, and develop problems and possibilities in their historically concrete local practice in encompassing societal relations. I have tried to show why it is that in order for analytic concepts and methods to be used that way, they must be based on a generalized science of the subject, articulated from participants' interrelated positions and perspectives in practice.

This holds for the conception of research practice, scientific subjectivity, and knowledge, too. In practice, research is founded on its particular prior knowledge of, connections with, and participation in the problems and possibilities of the practice it studies. If that were not so, it could not reconstruct a practice from its participants' first person standpoints (from which participants, hopefully, are to put the results to use). The research may miss its target, i.e. the practice as performed including its problems and scopes as experienced. Risks of being taken in by widespread mystifications about a practice, as its practitioners themselves see and perform it, may be countered by acknowledging that research is a special social practice with a special epistemological approach and particular interests, goals, and tasks in relation to the area of practice it studies.

References

Dreier, O. 1993: *Psykosocial behandling. En teori om et praksisområde*. København: Dansk psykologisk Forlag.

Holzkamp, K. 1983: *Grundlegung der Psychologie*. Frankfurt/M.: Campus Verlag.

Leont'ev, A. N. 1978: "The Problem of Activity in Psychology". In: *Activity, Consciousness and Personality*. Englewood Cliffs, NJ: Prentice Hall.

PUBLICATIONS 1992-1993
BY RESEARCHERS AT PSYCHOLOGICAL
LABORATORY & INSTITUTE OF CLINICAL PSYCHOLOGY
UNIVERSITY OF COPENHAGEN

Aboulafia, A., Nielsen, J. & Jørgensen, A. Helms
(1993) *Evaluation report on the "EnExl" Design Workshop*, 25 p.

Aboulafia, A., Jørgensen, A. Helms & Nielsen, J.
(1993) Modelling in user interface design: Designers' views of applications and requirement. In: *Proceedings of the 16th IRIS: Information Systems Research in Scandinavia*. København, Datalogisk Institut. 298 p.

Aboulafia, A., Nielsen, J. & Jørgensen, A. Helms
(1993) The ambiguous reality and formal methods in user interface design. In: *Proceedings of INTERCHI'93 Research Symposium, Amsterdam, 23-24 April 1993*. New York, ACM

Aboulafia, A., Nielsen, J. & Jørgensen, A. Helms
(1992) *The Person-Centered concept of observation in research in psychology*. The fifth Forum for the Person Centered Approach in psychology. 15 p.

Andersen, S.B.
(1992) The Person-Centered Concept of Observation in Research in Psychology, in: *Fifth Forum on the Person-Centered Approach, Book of Abstracts*, Terschelling.

Andersen, S.B. & Merrill, C.
(1993) Person-centred Expressive Therapy: an outcome study. In: David Brazier (ed.) *Beyond Carl Rogers*. London. 19 p.

Andersen, S.B. & Merrill, C.
(1993) A Content Analysis of Person-Centered Expressive Therapy Outcomes. In *Humanistic Psychology*, vol. 21, no. 3.

Arcel, L.T., Mantonakis, J., Petersson, B., Jemos, J. & Kalliteraki, E.
(1992) Female suicide attempt and shame. A cross-cultural comparative study of Greek and Danish women., *Culture, Medicine and Psychiatry*. p. 60f.

Arcel, L.T., Mantonakis, J., Petersson, B., Jemos, J. & Kalliteraki, E.
(1992) Suicide attempts among Greek and Danish women and the quality of their relationships, husbands and boyfriends. *Acta Psychiatrica Scandinavia.* 85, p. 189-195.

Axel, E.
(1992) One developmental line in European Activity Theories. *The Quarterly Newsletter of the Laboratory of Comparative Human Cognition.* 14,1, p. 8-16.

Axel, E. & Nissen, M.
(1993) Relating the Subject and Society in Activity – is Activity Theory becoming a Clotty Gravy? In: N. Engelsted, M. Hedegaard, B. Karpatschof & A. Mortensen (eds.) *The Societal Subject, Essays in Activity and Personality.* Århus, Aarhus University Press p. 67-83.

Bargatzky, T. & Kuschel, R.
(1992) (eds.) *The cultural construction of nature.* München, Verlag Peter Langs.

Bjerg, K., van Rijn, F. & Frerk, K.
(1992) Perspective on Home-Oriented Informatics and Telematics. In: *Education and society – Information processing 92 vol 2.* Amsterdam, Elevier Science Publ. p. 14f.

Borg, K.
(1993) Family life and flexible working hours. In: S. Carlsen og J. Elm Larsen (eds.) *The equality dilemma.* København, Ligestillingsrådet p. 67-79.

Bundesen, C.
(1992) *A computational theory of selective attention in vision.* Brain and Mind: A Commemorative Symposium, Det Kongelige Danske Videnskabernes Selskab, Smal papers.

Bundesen, C.
(1992) Concept of visual sensation in a theory of visual attention: A theoretical note. *Perceptual and Motor Skills.* 74, p. 874.

Bundesen, C.
(1992) *Predicting selection probabilities in race models by the Luce choice rule.* The Fifth Conference of the European Society for Cognitive Psychology, Paris 1992.

Bundesen, C. & Larsen, A.
(1992) The efficiency of holistic template matching in recognition of handwritten digits. In press. *Psychological Research/Psychologische Forschung.*

Bundesen, C.
(1992) The relationship between independent race models and Luce's choice axiom. In press. *Journal of Mathematical Psychology.*

Bundesen, C.
(1993) The notion of elements in the visual field in a theory of visual attention: A reply to Van der Velde and Van der Heijden (1993). *Perception & Psychophysics.* 53, p. 350-352.

Bundesen, C.
(1993) The relationship between independent race models and Luce's choice axiom. *Journal of Mathematical Psychology.* 37, p. 446-471.

Dreier, O. & Jensen, U. Juul
(1992) (eds.) *Action Health Research.* Århus.

Dreier, O.
(1992) Client Perspectives and Uses of Ongoing Psychotherapy. In press. In: O. Dreier & U. Juul Jensen (eds.) *Action Health Research.* Århus.

Dreier, O.
(1992) *Psychotherapy and Life-world.* Foredrag ved forskeruddannelseskursus, "Narrativity in Human Science Research", Sønderborg 1992, 8 p.

Dreier, O.
(1992) Re-Searching Psychotherapeutic Practice. In: S. Chaiklin & J. Lave (eds.) *Understanding Practice.* New York, Cambridge University Press.

Dreier, O. & Lave, J.
(1992) *Subjects in Social Practice.* In press.

Dreier, O.
(1992) User Perspectives in Change During Treatment In: P.B. Andreasen, E.H. Hansen, I.A. Lunde & H. Timm (eds.) *The User Perspective in Health Services Research.* København. In press.

Duke, D., Shum, S.B. & Jørgensen, A. Helms
(1993) Computer Entry Readout Device. In: *Internal AMODEUS Report.* York, University of York.

Duncan, K.D. & Prætorius, N.
(1992) Display Design for Fault Diagnosis in Complex Process Plant. *Ergonomics.* In press.

Duncan, K.D. & Prætorius, N.
(1992) Flow displays representing complex plant for diagnosis and process control. *Reliability Engineering and System Safety.* 36, s.239-244.

Engelsted, N.
(1992) A Missing Link in AT? *Multidisciplinary newsletter of Activity Theory.* 11, p. 49-54.

Engelsted, N.
(1992) *Two fundamental forms of behavior?.* 25th International Congress of Psychology, Paper.

Engelsted, N.
(1993) At a crossroads – An introduction. In: N. Engelsted, M. Hedegaard, B. Karpatschof & A. Mortensen (eds.) *The Societal Subject, Essays in Activity and Personality.* Århus, Aarhus University Press p.1-17.

Engelsted, N., Hedegaard, M., Karpatschof, B & Mortensen, Aksel.
(1993) (eds.) *The Societal Subject, Essays in Activity and Personality.* Århus, Aarhus University Presss.

Gade, A.
(1992) A nordic network for exchange of neuropsychology literature reference data. Presented at the 13th INS European Conference, Durham, July 8-11, 1992, *Journal of Clinical and Experimental Neuropsychology.* 13, p. 320f.

Gade, A.
(1992) Imagery as a mnemonic aid in amnesia patients: Effects of amnesia subtype and severity. In: J. Riddoch & G. Humphreys (eds.) *Cognitive Neuropsychology and Cognitive Rehabilitation.* London. In press.

Gade, A., Bohr, V. Bjerrum, J., Udesen, H. & Mortensen, E.L.
(1992) Neuropsychological sequelae in 91 cases of pneumococcal meningitis. In press. *Developmental Neuropsychology.*

Gade, A.
(1992) Neuropsychological sequleae in 91 cases of pneumococcal meningitis. *Developmental Neuropsychology.* 8, p. 447-457.

Gammelgaard, J.
(1992) *The tragic emotions.* The Third Delphi International Psychoanalytic Symposium.

Gammelgaard, J.
(1993) They suffer mainly from reminiscences. *Scandinavian Journal of Psychoanalysis.* 15, 2, p. 104-122

Hjæresen, O., Hedegaard, O. & Jørgensen, A. Helms
(1993) Quick development of high quality applications in a standardized graphical environment. In: *Proceedings of COPE'IT'93, Copenhagen, 14-16 june, 1993.* København, Dansk Dataforening. 323 p.

Jørgensen, A. Helms, Due, B., L. Clarke, I. Cowers, R. Rivers & J. Nielsen
(1992) *Report on Workshop Studies.*

Jørgensen, A. Helms
(1992) *Summary report on Empirical Designer Studies.* København, Psykologisk Laboratorium, 8 p.

Jørgensen, A. Helms, Aboulafia, A. Shum, S. og Hammond, N.
(1993) *Transferring and assaying design expressions in use.* 96 p.

Karpatschof, B.
(1992) The Control of Technology and the Technology of Control. *Activity Theory.* 11/12, p. 34-40.

Karpatschof, B.
(1993) Societal Anomali and the psychological turn of the mass. In: N. Engelsted, M. Hedegaard, B. Karpatschof & A. Mortensen (eds.) *The Societal Subject, Essays in Activity and Personality.* Århus, Aarhus University Press p. 201-225.

Kuschel, R.
(1992) "Women are women and men are men": How Bellonese women get even. In: K. Bjørkvist et. al. (eds.) *Mice and Women.* Festschrift for Kersti Lagerspetz San Diego, Academic Press Inc.

La Fosse, J.M., Cannon, T.D., Møller, L., Schulsinger, H., Mednick, S.A., Schulsinger, F.& Parnas, J.
(1992) Neuropsychologiccal deficits in schizophrenia: Relationships with genetic risk, obstetric factors and computed tomography. *Archives of General Psychiatry.* In press.

Larsen, A.
(1992) On sensation, perception and thought: A reply to Rönnberg. *Scandinavian Journal of Psychology.* 33, p. 282-287.

Larsen, A.
(1992) Review of De Valois, R.L. & De Valois, K.K.: Spatiel Vision. *European Journal of Cognitive Psychology.* 5, p. 3.

Larsen, A. & Bundesen, C.
(1993) An adaptive pandemonium of templates for visual pattern recognition. In: C. Bundesen & A. Larsen (eds.) *Proceedings of the sixth conference of the European Society for Cognitive Psychology: Summaries.* København, European Society for Cognitive Psychology p. 5.

Lave, J., Duguid, P., Fernandez, N. & Axel, E.
   (1992) Coming of Age in Birmingham: Cultural Studies and Conceptions of Subjectivity. *Annual Review of Anthropology.* 21, p. 1-26.

Ljungstrøm, C.
   (1992) Needs, Perspectives and Policy Recommendations on Adult Education in Denmark. In: M. Wouters (eds.) *Adult Education in the 1990s.* Brussel. In press.

Mortensen, A.
   (1993) Notes on communication. Axtivity theory, and zone of peoximal development. In: N. Engelsted, M. Hedegaard, B. Karpatschof & A. Mortensen (eds.) *The Societal Subject, Essays in Activity and Personality.* Århus, Aarhus University Press p. 229-239.

Mortensen, E.L. & Gade, A.
   (1992) Linear versus normalized T scores as standardized neuropsychological test scores *Scandinavian Journal of Psychology.* p. 230-237.

Mørch, S. & Frost, S.
   (1992) *A case of applied youth-research.* In press.

Mørch, S.
   (1992) Youth in the process of social change. In: J. Hartmann (eds.) *Youth in a changing Europe.* Uppsala.

Mørch, S.
   (1993) Youth theory: A prerequisite of youth policy. The role of the Danish school and youth work. In: *Jeunes et politique, Ouverage collectif en preparation.* Paris, Editions Agence d'Arc.

Mørch, S. & Frost, S.
   (1993) Pedagogical intervention and youth development. Theory and praxis in a pedagogical youth-evaluation project. In: N. Engelsted, M. Hedegaard, B. Karpatschof & A. Mortensen (eds.) *The Societal Subject, Essays in Activity and Personality.* Århus, Aarhus University Press p. 273-296.

Nielsen, J. & Jørgensen, A. Helms
(1992) *Designing User Interfaces: Intuitive Solutions and Imagination.* Proc. CHI'92 Research Symposium, Monterey 1992.

Parnas, J., Cannon, T.D. Jacobsen, B., Schulsinger, H., Schulsinger, F. & Mednick, S.A.
(1992) Lifetime DSMIII-R diagnostic outcome in offspring of schizophrenic mothers. *Archives of General Psychiatry.* In press

Petersen, A. Friemuth
(1992) *Flavia Moraro, On the Evolution of Gestural Language in Europe: A Historical Review of the Latin Influence and a Comparative Study relating the Italian and the Danish Gestural Tradition.* København, IAAS + Psykologisk Laboratorium. 105 p.

Petersen, A. Friemuth
(1992) *Les besoins de l'Home, leur évolution an cours des differents âges de la vie.* Institutpublikation. 16 p.

Petersen, A. Friemuth
(1992) On Emergent Pre-Language and Language Evolution, and Transcendent Feedback from Language Production on Cognition and Emotion in Early Man. In: J. Wind & B. Chiarelli (eds.) *Language Origin: A Multidisciplinary Approach.* Dodrecht, Kluwer Academic Publishers, p. 449 -464.

Petersen, A. Friemuth
(1992) *On Situational Logic as a Method in a World of Propensities.* PPE-Lectures, Universität Wien. 12 p.

Petersen, A. Friemuth
(1992) *Why man began to speak: On possible feedback effects of spech on individual levels of emotion and anxiety.* Institutpublikation, 21p.

Petersen, A. Friemuth
(1993) Aspects biopsychologiques de l'individuation: Individualité biologique, personalité et soi. *Les cahiers du Cerfee.* p. 71-89.

Poulsen, Arne
(1993) Activity and the disembedding of human capacities in modernity. In: N. Engelsted, M. Hedegaard, B. Karpatschof & A. Mortensen (eds.) *The Societal Subject, Essays in Activity and Personality.* Århus, Aarhus University Press p.141 -165.

Rasmussen, O. Elstrup
(1993) Conceptualizing fundamental social procesess. The path to the comprehension of entrepreneurship? In: N. Engelsted, M. Hedegaard, B. Karpatschof & A. Mortensen (eds.) *The Societal Subject, Essays in Activity and Personality.* Århus, Aarhus University Press p. 165-200.

Schultz, E.
(1992) Methods, Focus on Interest and Theory in Humanistic Research. In: N. Engelsted, M. Hedegaard, B. Karpatschof & A. Mortensen (eds.) *The Societal Subject, Essays in Activity and Personality.* Århus, Aarhus University Press. p. 109-131.

Shibuya, H.
(1992) *Modeling efficiency of visual selection: Partial report in duplex condition and in conjunction condition.* In press.

Shibuya, H.
(1992) Ningen no shikaku-jouhou-shori-katei: Sono seigen to sentakusei. In: Y. Hakoda (eds.) *Ninchi-kagaku no Furontia III.* Tokyo, Saiensu-sha. In press.

Stenvig, B. & Leth, I.
(1992) *Juvenile Sex offenders, a neglected problem?.* The Third Nordic Youth Research Symposium, 1992, 8 p.

Terrins-Rudge, D. & Jørgensen, A. Helms
(1993) Supporting the Designers: Reaching the Users. In: P.F. Byerley, P. J. Barnard & J. May (eds.) *Computers, Communication and Usability: Design Issues Research and Methods for Integrated Services.* Amsterdam, Elsevier. 10 p.

Willanger, R.
(1992) Neuropsychological syndromes and Awarness. In: *D. Vid. Selsk. 250 års jubilæumsskrift.* København. In press.

Willanger, R.
(1993) Theories of consciousness with special reference to methods in research. In: *Proceedings of the sixth conf. of the european Society for cogn. psychology.* København.

Willanger, R.
(1993) Theories of consciousness with specific reference to rehabilitation. In: *Symposium: Neurorehabilitation: Eine perspektive für die Zukunft.* p. 11.

Østergaard, L.
(1992) (ed.) *Gender and development. A practical guide.* London, Routledge.

Østergaard, L.
(1992) *Gender and helth. Module 3.* Gender and Third World Development, Brighton, Institute of Development Studies. 65 p.

Østergaard, L.
(1992) Health. In: L. Østergaard (ed.) *Gender and development. A practical guide.* London, Routledge p. 61-80.